# IT SHOULDN'T HAPPEN
# TO A MISSIONARY

*The All Nations Series*

All Nations Booklets aim to:

1. Provide basic teaching on various aspects of mission
2. Raise awareness of the importance of mission in Western churches
3. Stimulate support for mission through prayer and action
4. Help churches in the multi-cultural West to learn from the experiences of churches worldwide

# IT SHOULDN'T HAPPEN
# TO
# A MISSIONARY

## ALF COOPER
Jane Collins

MARC
SOUTH AMERICAN MISSION SOCIETY
ALL NATIONS CHRISTIAN COLLEGE

First published 1993
Reprinted 1995

*Front cover illustration*
*Taffy Davies*

ISBN 1 85424 168 0

**British Library Cataloguing in Publication Data**
A catalogue record for this book is available from
the British Library.

South American Mission Society
Allen Gardiner House, Pembury Road,
Tunbridge Wells, Kent, TN2 3QU

All Nations Christian College
Easneye, Ware, Herts SG12 8LX

Production and Printing in England for
MONARCH PUBLICATIONS
Broadway House, The Broadway
Crowborough, East Sussex TN6 1HQ
by Nuprint Ltd, Harpenden, Herts AL5 4SE

# CONTENTS

Foreword 7

Introduction: Painting Policemen is Wrong 9

1 On a Spanish Road 15

2 Dodging the Labels 33

3 Evangelist With 'L' Plates 47

4 Caribbean Break-Through 63

5 Who Needs Bible College? 77

6 Chile Para Cristo! 95

7 Where the Path Peters Out 109

8 From Mono to Stereo 123

9 Stocktake UK 139

10 Churches, Churches, Churches 147

# FOREWORD

'We'll take over the night-club', Alf said to me and to the other All Nations students with me. His actions fitted his words. We were on the overnight ferry to Denmark where we were invited to do a speaking tour. Alf sat in a corner of the ship's small nightclub, played his guitar and sang modern Christian songs. The young people soon forgot the dreary piped music and turned it off as they congregated round Alf. For three hours the All Nations team entertained the crowd with songs interspersed with short testimonies and words of witness. The following morning our cabin was besieged with youngsters demanding that we continue on the upper deck, so the whole morning was spent in lively evangelism by song and word until we docked in Esbjerg. As his college tutor it was clear to me that Alf had an unusual gift in evangelism and personal witness.

Alf's unbounded enthusiasm and love for the Lord may sometimes lead him beyond the boundaries of normal Christian wisdom, but I have found that his prayerful humility and intellectual ability usually temper this with sound biblical principles. In particular it has been good to see how Alf has fitted his dynamic evangelism and church planting within the firm boundaries of the Anglican church in Chile. This has given him the advantages of wise oversight, clear biblical traditions and the networks of an older denomination. Over the years of his ministry in Chile he has been used of God to develop practical systems of teaching and training, so that his churches should not only mirror his enthusiasm but also produce godly and mature Christian leaders.

Some of us may be tempted to laugh or even to shudder at some of Alf's approaches, but I am convinced that we all have much to learn from what God has done in and through him. And in the Lord's wonderful grace Alf is a man whom the Holy Spirit has used in tremendous ways. He has planted churches both in upper class areas of the city and also in the poverty of Chile's shanty-towns. The new believers who have formed these new churches have been so taught and discipled that they themselves now take a vital part in the leadership and evangelism of God's church in Chile. This is missionary work at its best and it is my prayer that it will inspire many readers of this book to move out into all the continents of the world in effective church planting and discipling mission.

I have thoroughly enjoyed reading this book. It's a good laugh and so easy to read, but its lively style cannot hide the deep spiritual lessons with which Alf's story challenges us. Once you have read this book, you will not quickly forget it.

*Martin Goldsmith*

# INTRODUCTION:
# PAINTING POLICEMEN IS WRONG

For many years I went once a week to preach in the central square in Santiago, capital of Chile. A Chilean pastor often came with me as a normal part of his training.

One night stands out in my memory, a night quite different from hundreds of other occasions: more nerve-wracking, more foolhardy and more mind-blowing. It was a turning-point in my understanding of evangelism.

I was feeling rather depressed as we set up our speakers on the Passeo Ahumada, an open paved area right at the heart of Chile's capital. We noticed there were more people around than usual, which lifted my spirits a little. Roger preached first, and as he did, a chant began all around, political slogans rising in a wave of sound. He glanced at me for guidance, but carried on: this sort of thing was not unknown, and we seldom had the luxury of preaching to a silent group.

Suddenly the military police appeared with sub-machine guns, and the crowds scattered. The police knew, even if we didn't, that a massive demonstration had been organised for just this spot. Roger wound down and dribbled to a standstill: his audience had vanished into thin air. My depression returned with a thump.

'What are we offering Chile?' I agonized to myself. 'How can the gospel be relevant here, where social reform is desperately needed, where injustice and inequality scream from all sides. We offer them Christianity. It's like giving aspirin to someone with terminal cancer.'

Yet the very hopelessness of the situation caused something to stir deep within me, and I knew this was a test case for God. In my heart, God was on trial. Perhaps, in God's heart, I was on trial too.

With a certainty I couldn't have had if I had stopped to think, I went up to the man in charge of the police, ignoring his sub-machine gun.

'Look,' I reasoned with him, 'don't chase the crowd away: I want to preach to them. They need the gospel of Jesus. I'll take the consequences.'

He looked at me, not unkindly.

'You're mad,' he said. 'They're just using you. You're an excuse for them to get going. You do realise that, don't you?'

'Please,' I insisted. 'Hold back your dogs and give me a chance.'

To my amazement, he agreed, and I got up and started preaching. The crowds came back, drawn by the sight of the passive military presence, perhaps, but the chant dying away as they fell silent and listened to the message. Soon there were two thousand or more, police mingling with demonstrators, and as far as I could see from my platform, their faces were turned towards me.

'What exactly is your life worth?' I launched into the message I had prepared. 'Ask a scientist. He will tell you that your body, reduced to the constituent chemicals, would have the market value of a few loaves of bread. But it wouldn't be worth doing, because the process would cost more than the results are worth. Materialism, then, is no use: it devalues you as people. You know you are worth more than that.' Some of the crowd saw a hint of political innuendo there, and approved with a grunt or a nod.

'What do your friends and family think you are worth? If you were kidnapped, what would they pay to get you back?' Now the clapping began. I was on their side. I stood on their behalf against the military police, who, amazingly, held their dogs and listened too.

'What about your enemies? What would they pay to have you killed?' A howl of approval went up. The chief agitators, clearly recognisable as a group near the front, started up the chants again, but they were ignored. They were no longer in control.

'You may not be worth anything to anyone, but God still puts a value on your life. Whatever you believe about God...'

'I'm an atheist,' shouted one of the agitators, no doubt peeved at the way he was losing face.

'OK,' I countered, pointing him out. 'Let me tell you what value God places on your life, as an atheist. I'll show you in two lines what God thinks of you.' Slowly I painted an upright line, then another through it to form a cross. 'God loved the world, and you, so much that he sent his only Son to die for you.'

I was gripped by the power, the simplicity and the

breadth of the gospel as I preached. I closed my eyes, and could have forgotten the crowd, they were so still. Then I looked again, and saw the sea of faces, dark Chilean features, some hardened and bitter, some puzzled, but each one of them dear to Christ. I preached my heart out, and when I stopped, all I could hear was the traffic in the distance.

'Let's pray for our nation, with its many troubles, and for ourselves.'

Next day it was reported in the newspapers. Both sides of the political divide felt vindicated by my words, and there were no reprisals.

That was the night I saw that the people of Chile preferred the gospel of Jesus Christ to politics. If there was an answer in Christ, they wanted to hear it. All they needed was someone to preach to them in a way that reached them. For me, that makes the risk worth taking.

Another day we were arrested when a different fellow-preacher, flustered by the militia questioning him, gesticulated enthusiastically with a paintbrush and flicked black paint into a policeman's face. We spent some hours in prison: not my first experience of being 'a fool for Christ'. Yet if it is for Christ, and if people discover God through me, even despite my foolishness, I will go on preaching.

Is Chile so different from anywhere else? I think not.

I regularly spend six months in the UK travelling around churches and sometimes take the opportunity of preaching in the open air. The response is different, perhaps less enthusiastic, but the need is the same, and people do respond.

Yet in many churches I plead with Christians to give evangelism a higher priority, and I usually meet a blank, a brick wall. 'How do we do it? Will they listen?' The unchurched seem more interested and motivated by the proclamation of Christ than the churched are by the opportunity of proclaiming him.

'I would no more defend the Gospel than I would a caged lion,' said Spurgeon. 'All I need is to let it out!' We are seeing today in the world-wide church, among the world's poor, deprived, oppressed third world, God's revolution for the twentieth century. Even in lands where there has been a socialist revolution, where man has done all he can to produce the 'perfect state', God is now bringing his own revolution.

'Everyone who calls on the name of the Lord will be saved.' Many will agree with that, but not all follow that thought through in the way Paul does in Romans 10:14,17. 'How, then, can they call on the one they have not believed in? And how can they believe in the one of whom they have not heard? And how can they hear without someone preaching to them?...Consequently, faith comes through hearing the message, and the message is heard through the word of Christ.'

Just as the cross was essential to the plan of God, so is the evangelization of the nations.

I have believed this for a long time, but it has taken many years and many painful mistakes for me to work out how it could be done. Now I want to share what I have learned, the embarrassing and the glorious all muddled up just as I lived it. If you can see how I reached my conclusions I hope you will try to apply them in your life and the life of your church.

Leave space for God! God is able! If we make mistakes, he can teach us. I know, because I've made most of them. God can use 'bad' evangelism. What he can't use is no evangelism at all. What he wants, of course, is carefully thought-out, prayerfully prepared, Spirit-led evangelism. If this book speeds up the learning process for a few people, it will have served its purpose.

*Gloria a Dios!*

CHAPTER ONE

# ON A SPANISH ROAD

The road between Segovia and Avila was cool and deserted that July morning. For a hitch-hiker it meant a moment for reflection...even prayer:

'God,' I began, 'I don't know if you are there or not, but if you are...' I faltered. I wasn't used to praying. The emptiness of the road seemed to reflect the empty longing within, reaching out for...what? who? 'If it's true what they said and you can hear me, forgive me, if my life has meaning to you...'

My mind struggled to come to terms with the idea of a God who cared about me.

Brought up in Chile, where my father worked with Shell, I led the sheltered and idyllic life of the Anglo-Chilean community. Then, when I was eight, my father died. My faith as a Catholic, deeply ingrained though it was, couldn't help me to come to terms with this loss. How could God let this happen to me? I lived with the contradiction, and the only certainty was that I had to fulfil the dream he had never lived for himself by going back to England for my education. So at thirteen I was packed off to a Catholic boarding school in the West Country.

Here was a new aspect of Christianity to digest: trudging in single file to Mass, down corridors the colour and smell of cabbage, walking like robots out of the sunlight and birdsong of the courtyard into the gloom of chapel and organ, the Headmaster moving gravely in his Benedictine robes towards the altar.

In my early years there I swallowed all the religion they taught, and did the rounds of Complines, Benedictions and Masses. I tried to take the retreats seriously, even though I inevitably seemed to be sent to the 'Sin Bin' for desecrating the silence with stifled laughter or bored kicking of the chair leg. For most boys, Confirmation was just part of the rigmarole, but I wanted it to mean something. I wanted God to mean something. Perhaps if I followed the path laid down by the school, God would appear through the boring trappings with which he seemed to hide himself. He didn't.

Meanwhile, my family's links with Catholicism were weakened. My mother, still in Chile but re-married after my father's death, had become a Jehovah's Witness, and my sisters were following her. This seemed like blatant indoctrination. Religion held no more appeal after that.

So I applied myself instead to learning what you had to do and say to be socially acceptable at school. You had to be daring, to dabble in drugs, spend your money on Rolling Stones LPs and hint at great successes with girls on the occasional trips up to London for the weekend. With my imagination and flair with words it was easy to cook up the sort of supremely confident character I wanted to be. If reality was a few steps behind the facade, then that was understood as well.

Meanwhile I was quite enjoying lessons, as I was able to specialise in languages and ramble around in the foothills of philosophy. Anouilh, Sartre and Camus introduced me to the view that it was not only all right to dispose with God, but that you weren't truly human until you did. This was heady stuff. What freedom! So while I outwardly chanted Psalms, inwardly passages of my set books would run through my mind. *The Plague* by Camus, for example. 'Since the world is set up in such a way that death controls everything, perhaps it's better for God if we don't believe in him, but just struggle against the forces of death without raising our eyes to heaven where he sits in silence.'

By the time I left school I had crossed the threshold from Catholicism to what I understood of existentialism. I traded a personal God for the vision of myself as the lone existentialist on a noble quest to find truth and meaning in an empty universe. And of course when that got a bit heavy there were always Dylan, the Stones, and the wider social prospects of university life to console me. Everything modern was good, and everything else was thrown out, including of course Catholicism, ritual, and all forms of Christianity.

Because I enjoyed studying, I applied to university and was accepted by Bristol to read Spanish, a subject in which I had a good start since I had spent my pre-school years in Chile. The social skills of school stood me in good stead here, and I was soon in the 'in crowd', having fun. There were problems too: the whole girlfriend thing never really turned out as it was meant to— it always seemed to be rather strained and traumatic, and the fulfilment I thought it would bring never happened, leaving me isolated.

I swung myself whole-heartedly into whatever was going on, and any system which tried to make sense of life was worth looking into. The political scene was alive in the 60s, and I got involved in a take-over of the Union building for some cause or other. With a bunch of friends I broke into an office and emptied a filing cabinet all over the floor. At the time it seemed a good thing to do, but I was the last one out of the room, and as I paused and looked back, I thought of the poor woman who would have to put it all back. I closed the door quietly and thoughtfully. There seemed to be a nagging flaw in the Marxist analysis of things: **man** himself. The futility and hypocrisy of Marxism, even then, became slowly apparent to me. It was one thing to destroy unjust structures, but where in all the world could anyone point to a just society that Marxism had built? How could you build a just society? What was being human all about? What was the point of me? If religion was the opiate of the people, here at university it seemed to me that Marxism was easily close to being the opiate of the intellectuals.

Next, shaking off the persona of the Existentialist Humanist Marxist, I started thinking about the realm of spirit. I absorbed myself in Professor Zahner's book on mysticism, and Feuerbach on spirit as a projection of matter. When I heard some friends enthusing about Transcendental Meditation I was an easy convert, ripe for the plucking.

I went to the appointment they had made for me with their guru. On my way I remembered I was supposed to take some sort of offering. A few dandelions from the grass verge and an apple 'borrowed' from a fruit shop seemed to meet the case.

In a fairly ordinary terraced house I was met by a young woman with long hair and dreamy eyes who accepted my offering, sat me cross-legged on the floor and told me my mantra. It was meant to be a great secret that I should divulge to nobody else: it sounded like 'Ah-heem'. We repeated it several times, and then she drew me into a kind of meditative trance with her. I was to go away and meditate twice a day, just using my mantra and imagining that I was going down into a pool of peace.

This I did with gusto, and was quite startled by the results. It really seemed to work at first. I went round telling all my friends and enthusing about meditation, until they all knew I was a meditation freak. To be honest, apart from carefully avoiding stepping on daisies, I don't think it changed my life in any way except that I felt excited about it. A little more peaceful and thoughtful, my worldview plunged now into a form of Hindu pantheism. I began to think of God, to believe in him, and to speak about him, but in Hindu terms. God or god, personal or impersonal, that didn't matter to me. I was the drop of water flowing into the ocean, seeking the bliss of Nirvana.

About this time I went to a family wedding, and explained my new world view to my cousin Rosemary. While my mother was still living in Chile and I was at boarding school in England, it had been Rosemary's parents who had given me a home base. So although Rosemary was twelve years older than me and I hadn't seen her for a while, I still felt close to her. Also, she called herself a Christian, and had even gone so far as to marry a clergyman: surely she would have an opinion worth listening to.

In the event I was rather disappointed. There I was, all dressed up in my dove-grey hired tails with several glasses of wine under my belt when she took it upon herself to treat me to an impromptu sermon on the cross of Christ. To be so dogmatic about any one faith just wasn't on, and I gave her a pretty rough ride. I found myself thinking back to that conversation, though, especially after what happened only a few weeks later...

'Hey, Alf, you should have come last night,' Pete bounded up to me as we arrived at a lecture theatre together.

'Hadn't finished this,' I explained, waving an almost cubic paperback whose bright covers quite belied the stodgey grey of the subject matter. 'Still haven't, come to that. How does it end?'

'Oh, you don't actually have to know what happens,' Pete dismissed my book with vigour. 'Old Richards usually tells you the plot in the lecture anyway. You just have to know what it's about, and you'll never find that out from reading it. Just read the critics—there's three pages in here that sum it all up.' He opened a library book at the page he had turned down the corner of, and thrust it at me. 'But don't bother about that now. Listen, it was a real laugh last night. We had a seance.'

That caught my attention. I turned sharply to look at him, banging my thigh on a desk as I lead the way to an inconspicuous corner of the lecture theatre.

'I didn't know you believed in the supernatural,' I taunted him.

'Course I don't,' he snorted. 'I'm a paid-up, card-carrying atheist like you.' Having reassured the both of us on that point, he felt he had to add, 'Like I said, it was just for a laugh.'

So was the lecture, judging by the doodling that went on beside me for the next fifty minutes.

'Coffee', he sighed as the lecturer closed his notes and finished with a flourish. Coffee at eleven was mandatory, even if you had only had breakfast at ten. By the time the stampede to the counter had been pacified into something like a queue, my thoughts had shaped up as a proposition.

'Pete, how about if we have another seance, under strict scientific conditions, with only atheists allowed to take part, and prove that it's all a load of rubbish.' I was really intrigued by the possibility of the supernatural. 'I mean, it's crazy. How could anyone believe all this could work? We need to blow the idea out of the water with our own seance, on our own terms. What do you think?'

'OK, suits me.'

'So what do we have to do?'

That night, six hardened atheists sat round a table in a well-lit room with a glass and pieces of paper for each letter of the alphabet and the words Yes and No. We each placed a finger on the glass.

'Are we doing all right so far?' Pete asked the thin air. The glass began to move, settling on the Yes.

'I felt you pushing it, Terry. Let's not waste time kidding around. I want to do this seriously.'

'It wasn't me, it was Alf.' I knew I hadn't. I didn't want the thing to work. The recriminations raged for another five minutes.

'Right!' decreed Pete, master of ceremonies. 'This is

getting us nowhere. You all shut your eyes, I'll move
the papers, and Tom can ask the next question.'

'Is anyone peeping?' said Tom, in sonorous tones.
There were a few snickers, but the glass moved to Yes.
Another battle ensued. That first night was fairly
inconclusive, but it was intriguing enough to have several more evenings, usually ending up with scientific
discussions as to the nature of the psychic link we were
setting up.

One day I was in the library working, when suddenly I felt a curious pull towards Pete's room. I got
there to find three more of our gang of six, and one of
the others also said he felt 'called' but had ignored it.
We were getting deeper in, and it intrigued me.

'The strange thing is, that the more seriously you
take this, and the more you allow yourself to believe
that we are communicating with a spirit, the better it
works,' concluded Tom. He certainly looked serious
enough under his heavy fringe.

'See you again tonight, then,' said Pete. 'How about
ten o'clock?'

By this time the God Squad had caught on, and a
couple of earnest types in green anoraks dropped by
that evening to put us off.

'What you are doing is forbidden by God,' insisted
one, his hand hovering near a bulging pocket. Did he
have a Bible in there, or a gun?

'It's not that we don't believe it works,' soothed the
other, his Adam's apple bobbing with emotion,
'because you know it does. But it is evil, and you are
opening yourselves up to spiritual forces which can
destroy you.' They were nervous but sincere.

'Look,' I said, 'just leave us alone. You do your
thing...let us do ours. OK?'

'We'll be praying for you,' was their parting riposte down the corridor before the door slammed.

A few minutes later we were poised for action. But quite unexpectedly, when my finger touched the glass I was flooded with a tremendous sense of evil. It was nasty and overwhelming. All I could think of was somehow getting away.

'You know, I think I'm going to play the guitar for a bit,' I said, as coolly as possible. 'You just carry on.' But in the next room, I felt that tugging feeling again, which was becoming increasingly familiar. Curiosity and fear mingled to draw me back to the Ouija board. The glass was writing frantically, with the fingers only just following.

'Make Alf join in. Make him. Tell him to join in.'

My friends looked up at me pale and mystified.

I knew I had to do something against this. I stood there, watching, and without moving my lips, started praying silently the only prayer I could remember. 'Our Father, who art in heaven…'

The glass stopped dead. I kept praying without the others knowing, and now a tremendous pressure built up inside me. When I trailed to the end, probably missing out a few bits, the glass started to move slowly again, and the pressure changed. Somehow it was outside of me, in the atmosphere. This was the most real experiment with the Ouija I had tried. I prayed, and the glass stopped, I stopped and the glass started. Five times I repeated the experiment before I told the others what I was doing.

'Every time I pray, this thing stops. Weird! What's going on? I'm an atheist!' But my voice trembled a bit…

The fact that I had abandoned my bravado encouraged the others to do the same.

'It's really getting jittery, isn't it?'

'I've had enough.'

'I haven't been frightened like this since I was a kid.'

Eventually the know-it-all students, atheists to a man and scoffing at the idea of the supernatural at the start of the week, ceremonially burnt the papers one by one. Ashen-faced they smashed the glass, exorcised the room by holding hands and saying the Lord's prayer again and went to bed much chastened.

Later, lying alone in the dark in the same room, I had a little conversation with myself. The sound of my voice was soothing.

'Let's rationalise this... What I have done is to open up some mediaeval part of my mind to release these powers. Now, in that mediaeval part of one's mind, one prays, so what I should do now is to pray.' So I did.

'God, I'm sorry I've done this. Please forgive me. I promise you I won't do it again.'

Immediately a tremendous sense of peace came upon me, and I slept.

The end of the academic year arrived, and several from the Spanish Department had applied for places on a course in Spain. When I realised we would be meeting at Gatwick for the flight out, I immediately thought of Rosemary again. Her husband's parish was near enough for me to have lunch with them and catch the plane with the others. I thought this was a great opportunity: I needed quite badly to talk to someone about what had happened, and at least they had some conviction about a supernatural world. Not that I was about to swallow the sort of stuff her husband David was likely to fling at me. I just wanted a free and open debate.

On the phone, Rosemary was first delighted to hear my voice, then wary.

'Oh Alfred, I'm so sorry. It really isn't convenient. David has a terrible back pain, and needs to rest before the youth group, and there's so much going on I really don't think...'

'Don't worry,' I cut in quickly, to save her embarrassment. 'I was just going to ask you...have you ever been to a seance?'

'Why, has Hinduism petered out on you? You don't want to get involved in seances: you could get in way over your head.'

'That's the conclusion I came to as well. Perhaps when I come back from Spain I could drop in and see you.'

'Yes, of course. Just give us a ring.'

I was disappointed, but not for long. Five minutes later, she phoned back. She'd had a word with David, who was quite adamant that his back shouldn't stop me coming. What she didn't tell me was that it was the idea of me being involved in seances that convinced them I needed help.

As I started to go through the story with them over lunch, I felt quite awkward. It seemed so far removed from real life, from the sunny kitchen where we sat. My welcome had been so warm, and the soup and rolls so delicious, it seemed far-fetched to launch into the improbable world of seances. Yet once again, as I got into the description of my feelings, they echoed in my mind, tugging at me as though they had a life of their own. I was encouraged by David and Rosemary's silence, their attentive listening.

'I kept my promise to God,' I rounded off. 'The others couldn't resist trying again, but I dind't let them use my room, and I went off with other friends that night. I felt that was important. But I still don't know what to make of it all.'

David gave Rosemary a glance, sending her in to bat first.

'I'm sure that was the right thing to do, Alfred. Your instinct must have come from all that Catholic schooling, even though you've moved away from it. The question now is, when you rejected Catholicism, did you chuck the baby out with the bathwater? Isn't it time to give God another chance?'

'Well, I'm not sure I agree...' I wriggled uncomfortably. That was all too personal, too cut and dried. 'I want to know how to fit all this spirit stuff, which seems so real, into a whole world view. I mean, when I was into meditation I discovered that you can find peace in many ways, and that's all God is, surely—a sort of harmony with the universe.'

'If you want fifteen different answers to the God question, you'll find them,' smiled Rosemary. 'You haven't been through half of them yet. Man is always trying to reach God one way or another. What Christianity says is that God reversed that process. He reached out to us, and we're not going to find God truly until we listen to what he said to us in the person of Jesus.'

There it was again. That black and white, true or false absolutism I found so hard to stomach.

'The trouble is, is it really as simple as that, Rosemary? My Mum gets all her answers from the Jehovah's Witnesses, and it all comes out so pat. Most of the Christians I meet seem so smug. But you both went to

Oxford University. I know you're not fools. Surely you're not shutting yourselves into the "Christ is the only answer" box?'

'That all depends, Alfred, on whether you are going to travel for ever, or whether you want to arrive somewhere. Yes, it is intellectually sound to believe in "true truth". Christ **is** the truth. If you are really searching for the truth, when you find him you stop searching.'

'Well, I certainly need a whole lot more evidence yet.' I was fencing, holding them at arm's length, but that last thrust had gone home, and I needed time to recover. I pushed my empty soup bowl back. 'That was delicious. Thank you.'

Rosemary followed the cue, understood my need for a breathing space, and produced a chocolate cake. As the talk rambled around family matters, I had time to think about something that had nagged at me ever since I had arrived. At last I pinned it down.

It wasn't just the sunlight in the bright kitchen. It wasn't just the pleasure of being with Rosemary and her likeable curate husband. It was more than that. The whole atmosphere was drenched with another kind of light, like a holy presence. Perhaps my mind had indeed been opened to a new level of reality, but I couldn't ignore that light. It had the same quality as the peace I had discovered when I prayed. Probably David was praying, even now, I surmised, looking across at him. These people really seemed to live what they believed and they believed so...personally.

While I scoffed outwardly, inwardly I hungered at the possibility that they might be right. You don't get more unintellectual than saying, 'You must believe in Christ because he is the truth,' but could not God be beyond the grasp of my intellect? If so, how could I find him? How come David and Rosemary thought they had?

They didn't say much more about God that day. Although God, and therefore evangelism, was their top priority, they weren't strung up about it. They were quite happy to be links in the chain which lead to others finding God, and knew when to stop pushing. To them, conversion was always a miracle, always God's work, so they just did their bit and then relaxed. For me, on the receiving end at the time, this was most welcome, and I still try to have the same attitude now when I am talking to others.

David did, however, hand me a couple of books to read on the plane. The first was called *Runaway World*. That was rich: implying that I was running away. It was them that had buried their heads in the sand, wasn't it? Yet as I read it, it described very clearly what I had seen around me, the disillusionment in all the philosophy I enjoyed so much. All the time I was wandering around Spain with my friends I was dipping into this book, hoping they wouldn't ask me about it. I wasn't ready for questions. The pieces of the jigsaw puzzle were coming together, but only slowly.

By the time we were due to move down to Portugal for the university course, I had run out of money. While my friends caught the train, I decided to hitch hike, which I thought was a far better way to see Spain, anyway. By this time I had started on the second book David had lent me: Schaeffer's *The God Who Is There*. That book stopped me in my tracks. The author seemed to know my every doubt and anxiety, all the while giving me the loving answers I longed for. Everything seemed to point in one direction—Christ. Maybe there was 'true truth' as Schaeffer put it, after all...on the other side of a step of reasonable faith.

About ten o'clock of the second day of my travels alone, I stood outside Segovia waiting for a lift. My mind was reeling with the battering it had taken recently. I couldn't ignore the questions any more. Everything seemed to hinge on sorting out these thoughts. In the distance was a big mountain. Did the road have to go over that? Was it really there? If the existentialists were right, it might only be in my mind, or only have a subjective reality. If the road had to go over it, then it must have an objective reality. Suddenly in all this relativism, everything became clear. If God was there, and God saw it, then it had an absolute reality. God was the key. Schaeffer said that God was there, and if that was true, it removed the philosophical problem.

But if God was there, I had a further problem on my hands. If he was there, then why didn't I know him? Michael Green's book told me that it was my sin that stopped me knowing him. Man's nature...why was it capable of so much cruelty, greed, deceit? Could it be that the flaw was fundamental after all? History did seem to be tragically closer to *Lord of the Flies* than to *Utopia*. A line from Jean Anouilh's *Becket* had always stuck with me. 'Under the crown or under the mitre you will always find that self-satisfied conceit common to man.' Sin! It was our undoing... So if God was there, not only was the mountain real, but so was the sin, and what God thought about it was the only thing that mattered. In the back of *Runaway World* was a prayer you could use to tell God that you were sorry for the sin in your life, and that you wanted Christ to come into your life and forgive that sin. Suddenly I wanted to do that. I reached for the book to look for the prayer.

'Wait a minute! Think!' a voice seemed to rasp in my ear. 'What are you doing? If you give your life to Christ like this you're going to end up one of those cranky Christian freaks who goes around in a mac, and looks weird, and you won't ever be able to enjoy yourself again.'

I looked at the mountain again. I could go over the mountain, and see what was on the other side, or I could stay where I was. No contest. I had to move on. In the same way, I had got so near to testing the God hypothesis, I couldn't bear to not try it. There was a sort of magnetism going on here. Anyway, if it turned out to be wrong, and God didn't make any difference, I could forget it. No, I had to pray that prayer.

'But what about your friends? They're going to think you've really flipped this time!'

This one floored me for a moment, and I wondered if it would be better to wait until I was eighty. Then my pride reasserted itself. When had I ever waited for them to approve? I had always done exactly as I wanted before, and usually dragged them after me. Why should I hesitate now? If this was the truth, I had to know it.

So I prayed the prayer in the back of Michael Green's book. It didn't seem quite personal enough, so I finally managed to blurt out my own thoughts and feelings to whoever was really God.

'God, I don't understand all of this, but if you are there, I give you my life.' Then I repeated, with emphasis, and with all my heart, 'God, I give you my life.'

The moment I said this, it was as though glory exploded within me. I knew immediately that the real battle had been about submitting to the God I had instinctively known all along was there. Now I felt I belonged to God, that I was in his hands. The light I had been seeking was not only found, it was inside me, and it was glowing. Clean, freshly laundered, new life as in spring, joy with all the colours of the rainbow. I couldn't stay still: I jumped with the rush of joy.

'I've arrived! I've arrived!' I was glad no-one was around to see me, as I must have looked like a drug-crazed hippy. But this was no trip...it was absolute reality. I felt as though Jesus was just behind me. I knew it was Jesus of Nazareth, his risen presence, on the road with me.

Was I on a religious flip? No. I was perfectly level-headed. For some reason, I had packed a pocket New Testament, and now I pulled it out and started to read avidly. Despite my fair knowledge of the Gospels, it all seemed so new. The words glowed so much they almost burned.

Eventually, someone picked me up. We started talking about politics, and soon I was talking about Jesus. The next lift I got, the conversation was about medicine and football, but I was soon talking about Jesus. Suddenly everything was Jesus-orientated. I couldn't grasp how everybody couldn't see Jesus, why everyone wasn't a Christian. I couldn't understand how they could all live without him. No matter that I had managed without him for years! Come to that, why hadn't anyone told me before? My amazement at meeting Jesus, finding him to be real after all, became uncontainable, impossible not to share with anyone who would listen.

I didn't know this was evangelism—it was the most natural thing in the world. None of the evangelism theory I learned or taught later contradicted what I felt from day one. Every Christian should share Jesus. The joy is indescribable. Jesus' promise, 'I will be with you always' is in the context of, and arguably on condition of, the last commandment he gave: 'Go and make disciples.' Jesus is there in a special way when the Gospel is preached. If your faith doesn't bring you joy, go and give it away!

God was now so close. I prayed about little details on the journey. At the end of that first day as a Christian it seemed completely natural to ask, 'Lord, help me find a hotel.' Suddenly I knew: go to the end of this road, turn right and then left, and there will be a hotel. Incredulous, I obeyed, and there was a perfect hotel, reasonably priced, with a room with a wonderful view.

As I stood looking out and praising God, a band came and played right outside my window. It was as if God was saying, 'You've arrived, and here is the party I'm giving for you, my child. I want to show you just how happy I am that you have become mine.'

It was a love affair with Jesus, beginning there on that Spanish road. I just had to tell everyone I met: a group of students from Essex, people in bars, and especially the friends I had come with. By a coincidence I no longer believed in, I was led to catch exactly the same train as them several days after I had left them. Everyone seemed to listen, and to take me seriously. My friends agreed that I wasn't the same person they had parted from less than a week ago. If they didn't like the change, they just had to lump it, but mostly they were just bewildered. They probably hoped I would have calmed down by the time term started again. I knew I wasn't going to, but returning to university presented a new problem for me.

'Oh Lord,' I groaned, 'don't tell me I have to join the God Squad!'

CHAPTER TWO

# DODGING THE LABELS

So I returned to Bristol. But not to the Marxists, the spiritists or even the transcendental meditationalists.

'I am a new creation,' I wrote in my diary. 'Does this mean I must become a narrow-minded robot in a sports jacket bristling with middle-class prejudices? Surely not. Perhaps I'll feel differently now.'

I was lonely. Who were the real Christians?

'I feel the need to be with other believers,' I prayed that night. 'I know I should share my experience and grow, but Lord, does it have to be with these "Christians"? Show me what **you** call a Christian, and I'll try to be one.' That seemed a fair deal. God shook on it the very next day.

Walking through the Wills Memorial Building I saw Tony Grant. Tony was a New Zealander with whom I had spent many hours arguing over spiritual matters in general, as he was one of those irritating types who just wouldn't shut up about God. This morning I suddenly saw him as a brother, and loved him.

'I've discovered you're a cousin of Rosemary Prior,'

he greeted me, and the answer to my prayer couldn't have been more complete.

He asked what church I was going to, so I went round to his room, told him the whole story, and presented my dilemma.

'I'm a baptised Catholic, but the church here only reminds me of the bad bits of Catholicism, and I can't bear the thought of joining the God Squad. What sort of Christian does that make me?'

'Just Jesus's sort of Christian,' he replied. 'All the denominations are no more than human ways of organising God's church. As long as you belong to the "body of Christ", that's all that matters.'

That was the first of many long conversations, in my room, in his room, walking over the Downs. Tony befriended me, cared for me, bought me my first Bible, visited me, lent me just the right books at the right time, told me firmly when he found anything of which I needed to repent, and nursed me through the whole reorientation of my life. My circle of friends was changing, the devil was throwing every possible emotional and practical spanner in the works, and Tony was by my side through it all.

Most important of all, he taught me to pray. He wasn't content with just laying the foundations of how to do it, upon which I have gone on building over the years. Above that he grounded in me, while my love for Jesus was fresh and uncomplicated, the importance of discipline and of keeping the lines of communication open at all times. Under him, from very early on, I began to get up early every morning to pray. Soon anything less than an hour felt as though I was short-changing God. Short-changing myself, as well, because it was often a struggle to get out of bed, and sometimes a struggle to find anything to pray about after the first obvious list. Yet it was these difficulties which helped me to grow closer to God. All those noble words like Quiet Time, discipline, sacrifice—they were just the stepping stones to what it was all about: joy, love, and the precious presence of Jesus.

That was what got me out of bed on cold mornings. Sometimes I asked God to wake me early, rather than relying on the alarm clock, just to confirm that he wanted me to pray. The Devil, of course, could give me hundreds of reasons for not praying, or not just now: that's how I knew it was important to God that I did. Every now and again I would trick the Devil by setting the alarm clock an hour early, say six o'clock. So when Satan sent his minions round at seven to tell me how much I needed the extra sleep, they found me with a cup of tea, an open Bible and an hour's prayer under my belt, feeling great.

Tony set the model for me. That vital first year of discipling a new believer, now central to my church growth thinking, he lived out with me. At the time I just knew he was a true friend, with whom I could be completely honest, and who grounded me as a Christian. Although he did such a thorough job on me, there was nothing of the 'identikit Christian' about him, or me when he had finished with me. His method, if he was following one, was constantly adjusted for a tailor-made fit. This was just as well, because I had never had a conforming type of personality, and I wasn't going to start now.

For instance, I had hang-ups about the Christian Union, precisely because it did seem to consist of 'identikit Christians'. Many of my prejudices about sports jackets and middle-class values needed to be re-thought maybe, but Tony could see that I would find it difficult to have the sort of fellowship and teaching I needed while I was battling through it all. So instead of sending me to join the God Squad, Tony found me a home group which was part of a local church.

That group was full of thoughtful Schaeffer-type Christians, and they were studying John's Gospel, which was perfect for me. Even so, I often arrived thinking it was all too hard, and this would be the last time I came. During each evening I would change my mind again, so warmed by the fellowship and the love I found there, the patience and the respect they showed me while I blundered my way through the study. Often I had spent the day reading philosophies which laughed at the possibility of any God, let alone the God of the Bible, and I must have been a prize producer of red herrings. Yet nothing threw them, so I kept coming.

Gradually I felt the attraction of the Bible as well as the fellowship. Those passages from John glowed into love as we read them, and burned into relevance for my life. Just as the spirit of the Ouija board seemed to gain power if you took it seriously, so God's Holy Spirit was enabled to work as I gave my life more and more to him. But there the comparison ended: instead of being paralysed by fear and dread of the evil spirit, and drawn into dark areas beyond my comprehension and control, I felt that God was inviting me to follow him into a kingdom of light, where my joy and peace were always growing. In the early days a new Christian can be just like a toddling child: very sweet to the onlooker, and a delight to himself. Yet just like a toddler he needs watching over and careful feeding.

As a new Christian, I wanted to mark my commitment in some way. It seemed to me from the Bible that baptism was the obvious choice, and that the symbolism of dying and rising to new life could only be enacted by full immersion. My baptism into the Catholic church as a baby had meant nothing to me, and my friends persuaded me that it didn't count for anything. I wanted to please them, and to please God, so I signed up for the next baptism service at a local church.

On the appointed day I turned up at Buckingham Baptist Church in my jeans, mildly amused by the whole spectacle, but determined that if any blessing was to be had, I would conform to make sure I got it. I put myself last in the queue so I could listen to the other testimonies and see what was expected of me.

By the time it came to my turn, I was really fired up and eloquent, and someone in the congregation told me afterwards that the Lord told him as I spoke that I would preach God's word one day. Then I waded into the water towards the pastor. His face was glowing, and not only with spiritual expectation. I was the tenth or eleventh he had done that day, and he was getting pretty tired. As I went under, his foot slipped, and I could see we were going to sink together. I tried to support him, he tried to baptise me.... It was only when it was all over that I realised that in my efforts to keep him up, my right hand had not gone under the water. It was as dry as a bone.

There was a dilemma for me! What was I to do? I had been told in no uncertain terms that full immersion was the only proper thing. It was too late to go back and do it all again, but there I was with one hand unbaptised, and my right one at that! All kinds of absurd possibilities flashed through my mind: would I go through my Christian life with this sort of spiritual Achilles' heel, like a missing piece of armour? Should I dip my hand in when no-one was looking? Or phone the pastor during the week and arrange for a secret hand-baptism? All that sounded ludicrous, but the serious part of me so much wanted to do the right thing. As I prayed about it a few mornings later, God showed me that he wasn't into legalistic symbolism. My peace returned, and I was finally able to laugh about it. Problems about the mode of baptism never bothered me again.

Another issue facing myself and many others at that time was the baptism in the Holy Spirit. I knew I had the Spirit in me from my conversion, but I also knew that I hadn't had many of the experiences fellow-Christians were talking about. Was there more to being a Christian than I had appreciated? I'd heard a lot about speaking in tongues, and although I didn't like the idea of babbling rubbish, it seemed to be a good place to start, so in a very matter-of-fact way I asked God to give me that gift. A funny little word came into my mind, which I whispered confidentially to a friend over coffee next morning, expecting him to laugh.

He stared at me with his mouth open for a while. Then he said,

'You've never seen that word before? No, I can see you haven't.' He started flicking through a Bible. 'Yes, here we are, Romans chapter eight,' he grinned in triumph and passed it to me. 'End of verse fifteen.'

Still not sure that humiliation wasn't lurking round the corner, I scanned the words nervously. 'When we cry, "Abba! Father!" it is the Spirit himself bearing witness with our spirit that we are children of God.'

There was my 'funny' little word, Abba. This shook me deeply. I shut my eyes and listened to my heart saying 'Abba, Abba, Abba...Daddy, Daddy, Daddy'.

How good of God to give me a word with a meaning. He, too, was prepared to work around my personal hang-ups.

This contented me for a while, but it didn't go any further until David Watson came to take a Mission at the University. By this time I had overcome my own prejudices sufficiently to forgive the CU their peculiarities, and went along to hear him. After his teaching, a small group of us prayed that God would fill us in a new way with his Holy Spirit. I still didn't pray in tongues, but felt my heart was just bursting with love. Later, praying by myself, I felt a beam of light from God flowing through me and again that wonderful love. A few days later I was babysitting when I read about a man who just made noises and let God do the praying until the language was given to him. This sounded naïve, but I had nothing to lose, so I put the book down and did it. There was no spiritual earthquake, no great flood of emotion, but I did know the words were coming from my heart. I realised I wasn't making it up when I looked at my watch and saw I had been at it for over an hour. The process may have been naïve, and may not be applicable to other people, but God used it in my case. As I walked home that night I was aware of a new dimension of power in my life.

Praying in tongues soon became the foundation stone of my times of prayer. However difficult it was to start, a good ten minutes of tongues always got the praise flowing. I learned to use it too as a listening time, and so many of the other gifts of the Spirit grew out of praying in tongues. It was important, not really as an end in itself, but as a first step.

From my observation and understanding of the Bible I have come to see the baptism of the Spirit more as a dimension of power available to every Christian. Sometimes it is a crisis Pentecost experience following prayer and laying on of hands, but more often, in a climate where the Holy Spirit is manifest and active, we simply grow in our experience. The important thing is that we live out what is in Scripture, live and minister the Kingdom more and more like Jesus. Only the Holy Spirit can enable us to do this. We need all God wants to give us of his power and gifts for the fantastic task of building his Kingdom. And we need to give him more and more of us!

Like many, I couldn't point to any one experience of baptism in the Spirit, but certainly many glorious experiences as I have grown in the Spirit and worked under his anointing. I want all God is giving! But God knows your personality, as I had discovered, and your needs, and has chosen your situation, so there is no need to get too tensed up about the whole thing. Just trust him.

Now I spent my working days engaging in theological discussions with tutors who would tear down my God intellectually, and my evenings on my knees praying to that same God, and enjoying the lovely reality of Jesus' presence. On the social side there were pressures too: friends taking me down to the pub to get me drunk, only to be faced by me explaining, 'Look, I'm a Christian now. Praying is much more exciting than getting smashed out of your mind. Why don't you try it?' Gradually, my earlier friends slid from the picture, because I knew that I couldn't obey God while I was living their lifestyle.

Even the good friends I shared a flat with, who showed a lot of tolerance for this fanatic, and with whom I am still good friends, agreed that I should move out. I was swept by a tremendous longing to serve God and serve people. I wondered how Christ could be made real today. I helped set up something called the 'Magic Garden Club', with a humanist friend, John. Every Tuesday night his flat was thrown open to anyone who wanted to come, especially lonely people desperate for a bit of human contact.

Some of Bristol's weirdest social outcasts would turn up, and we spent the most amazing evenings. I had my first eyeful of horrible depression and loneliness. I discovered the sordid life of homosexuals who lived alone and went from partner to partner. I met the emotionally broken, who couldn't relate to normal society. I spent time deliberately listening to the ugly, the strange, the different, and every sort of marriage and family problem. These people would never have come into a church. Many Christians just don't have—and wouldn't want—access to them, but they fascinated me. I was impressed by John's caring, which seemed more real than many Christians manage, yet I could also see his own deep anguish of spirit without Christ.

This group led me into all kinds of adventures, as evangelism and love always do.

One day an actor friend from the Magic Garden Club told me about another group meeting in Clifton, a 'different' one. He invited me but told me in dark tones 'Be careful, Alfredo'. Once I got there I realised that I was into a satanic group. When I arrived they were practising a spiritistic seance. I sat quietly and just prayed in tongues. Suddenly a fully fledged battle erupted. A man shouted 'Stop praying!' One of the women shouted 'I have the power to destroy you!', and I felt Satan's evil power pressing in on me from all sides.

Back at home, I trembled all night in a cold sweat, and had terrible dreams. A voice kept whispering to me, 'You have lost your salvation. You are going to hell.' Indeed, I felt I was already in hell, completely cut off from God by the power of evil from that group that had cursed me. No-one had taught me how to use my faith or the spiritual weapons God had given me.

Next day, abandoning lectures, I went to the home of Terry Kelshaw, a local curate. His young son opened the door and his wife, hearing my request, emerged from the kitching saying, 'I'm sorry, it's his day off.'

Despite this unpromising start, I was so over-whelmed by the sense of love and security in that home, by the contrast with the visions of hell that had plagued me all night, that I burst into tears. Hurriedly I was showed into the study and given a cup of coffee to keep me going while Terry got up from his lie-in. Soon he had heard the whole story, complete with shudders. We prayed together, and as my fears allowed me to think again, he showed me that God knows that his people face this sort of thing and has provided the protection we need. Would I ever know the Bible as he did? Romans Chapter 8 was definitely written with me in mind. My feet were soon back on solid ground again. Yet Satan had one last attempt to throw me.

'Hah! You're OK here, but what about when you leave this house? That's when I'll get you!' So as I crossed the little garden in front of the church, God sent an angel to touch me. That's the only way I can describe it. I was flooded with glory. Every trace of darkness left, and I felt the most tremendous liberation. Never since then have I experienced the power of dark-ness in the same way, as though Satan had done his best to make me experience hell on earth, and learned that the direct approach wasn't going to wash with me. I learned that his best weapons are fear and doubt, lies and condemnation. Yet now I knew, with the certainty of that experience, that he was vanquished by the Word of God and the power of God.

That didn't end the story, however, because the 'mini coven' met just down the street from my flat, and I encountered these people quite often. With a small prayer group I prayed and prayed against their activities. God showed me a verse from Romans 12: 'Do not be overcome with evil, but overcome evil with good.' I understood from this that I was to love them. But I cried out to God,

'Lord, how on earth can I love a witch?' Yet I knew I had to.

The next day, coming home, I met the woman who had cursed me, walking along the pavement with her daughter. Resisting the temptation to melt into the crowd, I squared my shoulders, met her eye, and smiled.

'Hello, how are you?' I had thought this was a safe way to start the conversation, but she looked very startled.

'More to the point, how are you?'

'Oh, I'm fine, thanks,' I smiled.

'But I don't understand. The last person I put a curse on was in bed for months.'

'Ah, but this time you're dealing with a Christian. You should know you have no power over anyone God protects. What's more,' and by this point I found myself saying words which surprised me as much as they did her, 'I'm coming round on Sunday to take your daughter to Sunday school.'

Not text-book evangelism, perhaps, but God knew

what he was doing. I took the daughter to Sunday school regularly after that, and her mother seemed powerless to stop me. The leader of the coven raged, my Christian friends prayed and fasted, and eventually the coven was split by tremendous rows, and they all went off in different directions. Since then I have never feared Satan again, knowing him to be powerless before Christ. I don't go around looking for demons, but if I come across one, I step on it and keep on walking.

Meanwhile, back on the academic calendar, final exams were looming. I had taken some exams after the first two years, and my attitude at that time was that I was bound to sail through them because I was a Christian. I landed a third, only just a pass. That was what I deserved on the little work I had done, but not the best I was capable of, and I knew it. So forewarned, I pulled my socks up, burnt some midnight oil, and gave it my all. To my delight my final marks pulled the overall results up into an Upper Second. 'In matters of career, as well as the Christian life,' I wrote in my diary, 'some things come by prayer alone, and others need hard work as well. It doesn't show lack of trust in God to actually do some work, attractive though this theory has been to me!'

At this cross-roads in my life, of course, I needed some guidance. What next? A talk by someone from the Wycliffe Bible Translators really impressed me. They were so dedicated to the lost, to those with Bibles. And here was I, a linguist. How did I apply? I took the name and address of All Nations' Christian College, which they recommended, but before I got round to writing, also saw some leaflets on Voluntary Services Overseas. What a good way of testing my rather uncertain call to serve God.

Although I applied rather late, they accepted me, and gave me the choice of Chile or Montserrat. Chile didn't sound much of an adventure to me: I had grown up there. Almost before I knew it, I was jetting off into the sunset. Next stop, Montserrat, wherever that was.

Everything had moved so fast. I had hardly adjusted to the very public and dramatic change of becoming a Christian. How deep-rooted was my faith? Fellow-Christians talked about the challenge of 'real life', and one had warned me to beware of alienating people before they got to know me. Maybe I could give myself a year's respite. I could rest from the batterings I so often received when I tried to share my faith with others. No-one in Montserrat knew anything about me, except that I had come to teach at the school. I could be anyone, run really wild. Fall in love with a dusky maiden and build a house of coconut palms at the edge of the pounding surf. Was my Christianity an optional extra for this year in the back of beyond?

I toyed with the idea for a while. Without the emotional high of new conversion, I was faced with a rational decision. But the answer was never really in doubt.

I had doubted my Christianity at school. I had rejected it at University. Then God had shaken me up and taken a hold on me. I didn't fit easily into the God Squad, but I was a Christian. I might have one hand unbaptised, but I knew I was his. I had taken my time to come into the fulness of the Spirit, but God knew I loved him. Satan had flung me into darkness for a while, but I had never left God's heart.

No, even if I could hide my faith in Montserrat, even if no-one ever knew the real me, God did. And I had to be true to him.

So as the plane circled and landed in Montserrat, my mind was made up. I was a Christian, and I would obey the command: 'Tell everyone.'

Both Montserrat and I were going to rue that decision on several occasions before the year was out.

# CHAPTER THREE

# EVANGELIST WITH 'L' PLATES

The heady rhythms of the steel band enticed me down the road, and as I grew nearer the smell of steaks cooking on an open barbecue added their magnetic power. Whether this really was a 'Welcome to Montserrat' party, or whether they would have had one anyway, I could see I was going to enjoy myself. It had been a long day, this first full day on the island, and I intended to relax.

As I came into sight, a doctor I had been introduced to earlier leapt out of his seat and launched himself towards me, somehow conjuring up a man with a tray of drinks in the same movement.

'Ah, Alf, isn't it? Help yourself to a drink, then you must come and join us.'

I looked at the drinks on offer. Long fizzy drinks and smaller, more serious-looking glasses faced each other in battle lines across the tray. My 'host' was clutching what I assumed to be a large rum, but I played safe and went for the fizzies.

'I can't tell you what that is, I'm afraid,' he waved

dismissively. 'Haven't touched one for years. Wife likes them though...' I smiled at the waiter to say thank you, but he had turned away, obviously quite used to being summoned and then ignored. Now I was shepherded across the room towards a group of three, a man and two ladies, who seemed deep in conversation. They were roaring with laughter, but when they saw us coming, they arranged their faces into suitable smiles.

'This is Bill, whom you met in the Staff room, I expect.' I must have looked puzzled, because Bill cut in quickly, 'No, don't worry, I haven't met you yet.'

'And this is my wife Debbie, and Bill's wife, Vera.' I shook hands all round, but my mind was already reeling with the information I had been given that day, and I forgot the names as they were said. I was so grateful to Bill who added, 'If I were you, Brian, I should leave him here for a while before you drag him off to meet fifty more people.' So, that's who he was—Brian. My mind had been struggling with the problem since I had seen him.

'If I do that, I'm afraid you will be subjected to intense cross-examination by the ladies until they know all about your pedigree, hobbies and ambitions. It's better just to say something quite awful and then they might leave you alone.'

'Not a bit of it,' threatened one of the two. 'The awful ones are far more interesting.' She smiled encouragingly at me.

'The plain fact is that the VSO's are anticipated and discussed like visitors from another planet,' explained Bill. 'Our little ex-pat community here runs out of real news pretty quickly, so they've got good at making it up. A new arrival is always exciting.'

I had expected this kind of scrutiny, and played my

part with gusto for the next ten minutes, until a Head of Department and a friend accused Debbie and Vera of monopolising me, and took them off to dance.

'Ready for a few more names yet?' Bill swopped my empty glass for another fizzy. 'Thirsty work, meeting people, I always think.'

Soon I was launched into the society which I was expected to join, by virtue of my skin colour and education. Theirs was a privileged life, focused on enjoying themselves, which they did very whole-heartedly and well. In some ways I felt at home, because the expatriate community of my childhood in Chile enjoyed the same unspoken assumption of superiority and the right to happiness. They were so friendly and helpful that it would have been easy to slot into the 'star category' prepared for VSO's.

Yet from the start I was uneasy. I only needed two or three of the 'ladies' drinks' to learn that they were far from harmless: my drinking days were far enough behind me for my capacity for alcohol to be quite low. Then there was the conversation, which seemed to be about nothing and went round in circles. The most exciting topics for them were speculations about whether so-and-so's wife really was still corresponding secretly with a VSO who had left under a cloud of suspicion last year. The best news I had for the day was the Good News I read in the Bible, but I somehow couldn't imagine drawing them into a heated discussion on the nature of the Kingdom of God.

Then Sunday came, and following instructions I set off for the Methodist church. This is where whites worshipped, I was informed. By the end of the service I had to query that statement. This was where whites met their neighbours, admired each other's clothes, sang a few songs and then drank coffee. Not one person seemed to have any spiritual insight at all, not even the minister. Whatever faith had drawn him into the ministry had been knocked out of him by a theologically liberal training, and he seemed to have lost his way completely.

On learning there was another meeting that evening, more informal, I thought I had better go along to see whether those who were keen enough to turn up twice a day had any speak of new life in them. I prayed a lot in the meantime for God to show me his people there.

The evening meeting was more like a Bible Study, except that it was a Bible dissection meeting. The minister explained away a couple of Jesus' miracles, and then deduced that God had never used miracles to draw us to faith, and didn't do miracles at all these days. I could take no more, and put up my hand.

'I've seen several healings myself,' I announced, 'and other miracles. I don't see any reason to doubt the gospel account.'

Shouts of 'Amen, brother!' came from a few old ladies at the back, but the minister flustered his way through some sort of response, just repeating what he had already said. Out of sympathy for him, I decided to leave him alone. I never went back.

During the following week, I fell into conversation with Howard Fergus, the Chief Education Officer, who asked how I was finding the island. That morning I had spent some time asking God what I was to do about church, and somehow I suddenly knew that I could confide in this man.

'I'm settling in very well, in most ways, but I'm a bit disappointed with the Methodist church.'

Howard's face creased into a lovely grin at my tactful understatement, and his eyes twinkled.

'Well, if you want to stay with your own people, there's not that much choice. But,' he lowered his voice to a conspiratorial whisper, 'if you'll give us black Pentecostals a chance, you'll find there's less coffee and more Spirit when we get together!'

Next Sunday, I discovered that Howard too was a man who used understatement. I had never been to a Pentecostal church. I was the only white person balancing on the wooden benches. Yet I didn't need to worry that people were looking at me. They had come to meet with Someone more interesting than me. The singing nearly raised the roof, and I felt the Spirit stirring within me as I joined in. Then they announced a time of prayer. I closed my eyes, waiting in the silence.

'Come, Holy Spirit, and lead us in prayer,' came a sonorous voice, and then the silence returned. I'd never heard a prayer quite like that, but I was just thinking how effective it sounded, when the prayer was answered. The Holy Spirit came, and those people prayed.

Gone, the reverent silence. Frayed at first by a few mutterings, and then punctured by several people praying aloud, together, from all sides, it was soon quite put to flight as groans, declarations of love and torrents of prayer in English and in tongues just poured out of the congregation. On one side of me Howard was on his knees. On the other side a man stood with his arms in the air, swaying dangerously with emotion. One lady was lying face-down with her arms outstretched, while somewhere behind me a bench was knocked over as people roared and raved.

Culture shock I had heard about. This was something else. Perhaps this wasn't a true church at all, but some sort of voo-doo gathering, with demonic practices going on. Yet it didn't feel like that. So, in the middle of the chaotic atmosphere I knelt quietly and whispered privately to God.

'Lord, what is this?' Simple prayers seemed the order of the day.

And a quiet voice in my heart said, 'Don't put your eyes on men, put your eyes on me.'

I did, and the unutterable sweetness of Jesus' presence was with me in such a way that I didn't worry about what I was doing, and whether I stood out from the crowd. From that moment, this was my spiritual home on the island. By the end of the year, when it came to letting go, I was worse than any of them.

God's Holy Spirit is the same all over the world, but our response to him is conditioned by the culture we live in. By leaping in one step from England to this, I had experienced both ends of the spectrum, and no spiritual context has taken me by surprise ever since. A great bully of a man drops sobbing to his knees, a teenager laughs and laughs, a little old lady thumps her fist into her hand in emphasis—and in them all, God is working. On Montserrat I learned what it was to be 'Shut in with God, man' and to move with the Spirit in many different ways. Some shake, some raise their arms, some jig about, and the less you worry about what you are doing, the more God can show you of himself. You can thump the bench, curl up in a ball, pray at full pitch, or be very very still, and God will always bless you if you put faith into your expression of love and praise to him. There was some very 'holy rolling' going on in that place.

And among those black Pentecostals were some of the holiest men and women I have ever met. Especially Sister Howes.

Sister Howes was the wife of the pastor, and they were a saintly and loving couple, a true man and woman of God. Often silent, Sister Howes could nevertheless turn a look of such holiness on you that fear of God came upon you. You felt you ought to be taking off your shoes. Mostly she was a sweet, loving mama, who joked and loved you as you were. But when she spoke with holy fire burning in her eyes, you heard God speak. When she preached, you quaked on the bench. She didn't just expound the Bible and apply it in general terms: she would move down the centre aisle, slowly, listening to God, and point at people, revealing their sin in public! Her source of information was clearly not local gossip, but a Word of knowledge from God.

'What about that letter, brother?' or 'What about the things you were saying as you walked home from church?' No aspect of our lives seemed to escape God's scrutiny. If ever we had been unaware that the Spirit came to convince and convict men of sin, we knew it now.

On one occasion there was a young girl standing by the door at the back, mocking at the 'ravers', as sometimes happened. Sister Howes paused and pointed dramatically until all eyes were on her. Then Sister Howes made a strange gesture over her stomach, signifying that she was pregnant. The girl was unmarried, and stormed off, furious. Nine months later she had twins. There was no way Sister Howes could have known before the girl did.

Oh yes, it was an adventure to go to church when

Sister Howes was in the Spirit. A holy adventure, and you walked carefully. As Sister Howes said to me one day, 'There are many ways in which men serve Christ, but oh, this Pentecostal way is sweet, so sweet.'

I understood just what she meant.

Unfortunately, joining the black church was a *faux pas* as far as the expatriate community was concerned. It just wasn't done. A VSO was automatically part of the white social elite, made up of doctors, lawyers, politicians and all that was loud and most prominent on the island. They were expected to fit into the everlasting round of drinks parties, beach barbecues, and dances. The Pentecostals didn't drink, and didn't dance, and although I had nothing against drinking and dancing personally, I felt my first allegiance was with my new church.

So when I was invited along with everyone else, I had to cause a stir by asking for soft drinks when all the men were drinking rum, and somehow avoid dancing. As a new man in those circles, this was quite difficult. At one of the early dances I was having quite a pleasant conversation with someone when I realised she was getting rather too friendly.

'I find these steel bands quite amazing,' I extemporised rather clumsily. 'I think I'll go and have a look.' She followed me across the room, and I could see that I was going to have to be blunt.

'I do hope you're not offended,' I shouted over the music, 'but I'm a Christian, and I don't dance.' She just stared at me.

'Well, I think it's a great shame.' She turned back to her husband, and didn't speak to me again that evening. For the next hour or so I watched her going from group to group saying something that made them all turn and look at me, until I could take no more and went back to my room.

'Lord, oh Lord,' I groaned with my head in my hands, 'I hope I've done the right thing. I've tried to make my position clear without causing offense, but it hasn't worked. The die is cast now. Please help me.'

From there things went from bad to worse. Having made my stand, I thought it would be easier to witness to these people. Yet increasingly I was regarded as a fanatic evangelical, and very insensitive. Several people went out of their way to avoid me. I felt such a burden for their souls, and cried out in prayer for them. I was torn in two, and often ended the day in emotional turmoil. The people I shared a house with more or less told me to shut up. So I went to my room, and read George Verwer, and Nicky Cruz, and Billy Graham, and longed to be all these great evangelists rolled into one. And the next morning, the agony would start again.

'Coming to the sailing club with us, Alf?' John had obviously decided to try again.

'I'm afraid I can't. It's Sunday.'

'Precisely.' His voice was patient. 'We always go to the sailing club on Sunday.' Then he realised compromise might be needed. 'You could come along after church, if you prefer.'

'I don't really think I can, John. You see, in our church we don't drink or socialise on a Sunday. I really think I ought to behave like them, since I am with them.'

'But why are you with them? What's wrong with the Methodist Church? Not good enough for you, I suppose. If you think you're going to spoil my enjoyment of a few harmless drinks by telling me it's sinful, then you're wrong.'

I tried to make myself clearer. 'I don't want to stop you enjoying yourself. It's just that the Lord means so much more to me than drink, and...'

He could take no more. 'You know what the trouble with you is, Alf? You think you're so much better than everyone else. Oh, I give up.'

Once again I retired to my room to pray and prepare for church.

My year on Montserrat taught me a lot about prayer. Thanks to Tony Grant I already had a habit of regular prayer in my life, but now it became a passion. It was easy to get up at six o'clock in the West Indies, and pray and read my Bible for an hour before breakfast. Then after school I would pray again, and while the others went to parties I would pray again for a couple of hours. An hour every week was spent interceding for England, and another for China, which was a place I believed God wanted me to pray for. John and the others would come home late at night in high spirits to find me groaning in prayer in my room, or on my knees in the living room. This only added to my reputation as a fanatic.

As if joining forces with the Pentecostals wasn't bad enough, I found the ideals which had made me set up the 'Magic Garden Club' now lead me to associate with the lowliest people on the island. You didn't get any lowlier than Johnny MacBrown.

Often drunk, usually barefoot, Johnny staggered around the island causing giggles and sneers and being called every sort of rude name. Beneath the rags and smells he had a heart of pure gold. He would bring me apples, and we went for walks together. We were both so lonely, and our friendship meant a lot to both of us. He lived in a little hut with banana leaves for a roof, very primitive and quite isolated. I came to love it there.

All this was quite unprecedented, and the news roared round the white community like a tornado, further blighting my image. Even the Pentecostals didn't understand my motives here. The man was a drunkard, paying the price for his sin, and quite unrepentant. Why waste my time with him? Their logic didn't stop my love for him, or for a few other tramps I saw occasionally. They were the laughing stock of the island, bullied and teased wherever they appeared. In the Third World the weak are spat on and ridiculed, and there was I beside them. Even I questioned myself at times, but always I reasoned Jesus would have been with these people, so why not?

To begin with I was shown some respect, or at least curiosity, in the staff room. I was the only white to get involved with the black people at their level, with no sense of superiority. There was quite a vocal black power movement on the island, so some of the coloured staff appreciated this move. Yet the most powerful blacks were often the richest and most influential people on the island, and they celebrated this fact with a lifestyle that I found difficult to respect. Although I tried to be sensitive about this, I felt I had to help them see that sin was sin, and that they needed a Saviour.

Coming from an Anglo-European, this was too much. They had been preached at by their own people before, and managed to escape from them into the liberal Western civilisation that the British brought to the island. Now along came a product of the civilisation they wanted to emulate, and he was thundering on about Christ and sin again.

'I don't see why a man can't have a bit of fun in and out, and if she's bored with her marriage it can help them both. What do you think, Alf?' I could tell that this tall, dark doctor was goading me, but I couldn't see any way round it.

'I think adultery is adultery, and adultery is sin, and even if there aren't any consequences at the time there will be pain later, and the judgement of God.'

'Well done, Alf,' said Bill sarcastically, drawing me away from the embarrassing silence which followed. When we were out of earshot of the others he explained, 'Didn't you know that Chris has been carrying on with Janet for months?'

'Not the Chris who was standing there?'

'The very one. Peter set the whole thing up. Quite clever really. But I don't think Chris is going to be your bosom pal from now on.'

I sighed. One more wouldn't make any difference. Dear God in heaven, does this situation look different from your perspective? Am I doing what you want me to do? Is it serving any purpose? They don't seem to pause in their complacency to listen for a moment, but perhaps they go home and think about it. Meanwhile, the only results I see are ostracism and cold-shouldering. Lord, I don't see how I can live any other way now. But just show me that this is what you want...

The hours I spent on my knees, alone, more than compensated for the pain, the cost of following Christ in the only way I could understand. My teaching was not going down very well, despite meticulous preparation, and everywhere I went I sensed this cold wall of hostility, and jeering and laughing at me behind my back.

The folk at the Pentecostal church were lovely, but they were Montserratian, and their culture was very different. I felt alone.

But I was alone with Christ. I always sensed Christ with me. During those hard first weeks I made many resolves to keep close to Christ, and never, never, stop praying.

Just before I arrived on the island, a group of people about my age, mostly girls, had been won to the Lord through the Pentecostal church. They were very keen, and met in the church to pray at lunchtime–every lunchtime. I decided to join them, although it meant there was no time to eat. I had been fasting on Wednesdays anyway, and going without lunch every day meant I was getting quite thin. My VSO friends started to worry about me.

'Alf, you need to look after yourself. This prayer thing is getting out of hand. You look green most of the time. Make sure you take something to eat with you. You're going to make yourself really ill.'

'Thanks, Alan. It's good to know you care. But don't worry. I'm doing it for the Lord, and he will keep me.'

He did. And those prayer meetings were very good. We were asking God to move on that island, to bring a time of revival, especially among the young people. We all talked about the situation in which we worked, and all drew strength and encouragement from our time together.

'It's really good that you can join us, Brother Cooper,' said Brother Housen as we left the church to head back to work one day. 'You move in such different circles from most of us, and bring a whole new part of Montserrat with you to be prayed for.' I looked at this tall, thin man, who lived all-out for God. His sincerity shone in his eyes, and he seemed to have no doubts or difficulties about anything, but he was becoming my friend and I decided to trust him.

'Well, I certainly feel more at home with you people than I do in the school,' I admitted. 'As a list of prayer topics, my contacts may sound impressive, but actually it's all rather hard work.'

'I'm sure it is, but we're behind you.' We walked on a few yards, while Brother Housen seemed to be debating something in his mind. 'Alf,' he said eventually, 'would you be interested in praying with us at another time?'

'I should think so. When's that?'

'Five o'clock on Saturday mornings.'

'Oh no!' But on further reflection it sounded good to me to have another challenge. So on Friday evening I did all my school work, preparation, homework correcting and set my alarm for four o'clock so I could have an hour of quiet time before going on to be at the church at five. One by one we'd trickle in and start praying, praying, praying.

The Pentecostals were wonderful pray-ers. If they wanted anything to happen, prayer was the top of their agenda. If things went well, they prayed. If things went badly, they prayed.

On Friday lunch-times when we went into the church it was always special. Sister Howes spent Friday there, fasting and praying all day, and the whole atmosphere was quite changed by her little figure squatted down in a corner. One Sunday she was what we called 'taken in the Spirit' and among other prophecies she said God was commending us young people, and that we must carry on because we would see the answers to our prayers one day. This really encouraged us.

And boy, did I need some encouragement. The aim of all these prayers was to see people won for Christ, but I knew I had to witness to my friends as well as pray. I longed for them to understand, to come to know the joy I knew, but I was useless at it.

Several times I read a passage from the Bible that really seemed to fit one of my friends in the house. Once I burst into Richard's room, and said, 'I just want to read you this. What do you think?' Then I read the passage, and expected to see some reaction. He just looked at me with pain and pity. Most of my friends respected my sincerity, but outwardly nothing happened to them, except a gradual turning away from all that was important to me.

Then God lead the church in a new direction. At one prayer meeting someone prophesied, commanding us to take the Gospel out to where the people were, in the market-place. In keeping with his character, Brother Housen leapt to his feet and said, 'I go'.

I reached out in my spirit to God, and knew my place was beside him. As I opened my eyes, I knew his eyes were on me, and as I stood up with him I felt the warmth of his smile. 'Me too.'

From then on, after the Saturday morning prayer meetings, Brother Housen and I would go out and preach in the market place. We called it preaching, but in fact we never got anything like a group of people to listen, so we would hand out tracts and try to draw people into conversation.

This was another thorn in the side of the dear white ex-pats to suddenly see me there making a fool of myself again. I saw them in the distance, but they rarely came anywhere near us, and if they did, they would look straight through me. So many of them did this, that I'm sure they had chosen this as a tactic. But they weren't the only ones. Nearly everyone did the same.

I had to admit that our evangelism was a much prayed-over failure. I was devastated. I cried out to God; I fasted; I searched the Bible. Nothing was going to make me give up. For six months I went all out for success, and met with nothing but failure. I did everything like the books said.

My life was nothing like the books.

CHAPTER FOUR

# CARIBBEAN BREAK-THROUGH

'Lord God, we ask you to break down the walls of unbelief we see around us, so that we can spread your word to these people…' Brother Housen was praying with quiet determination, but my heart wasn't in it. I glanced at his shining black face, so dear to me now, and wondered what it would take to shake him.

He was perched on a rusty oil drum in an abandoned corner of the market, with empty coke cans and banana skins around his feet. It seemed the right place for the two of us to be: round the back of a grubby fruit stall, where people threw their rubbish and things they wanted to forget about. No-one was in the least interested in the tracts we held, or in anything we said.

It was just like every other week. Two hours of victory-claiming prayer in the morning, grab an orange or two for lunch, then two hours of rejection and humiliation in the afternoon. I thought of the men I shared a house with, packing a sumptuous picnic while I wolfed my breakfast that morning, and even now sprawling on the sun-baked sand or cavorting in the breakers with their choice of the young ladies of the island. Why, when my rightful place was with them, did I condemn myself to sweating under the Caribbean sun, ducking crates of mangoes as they were shunted around the market, slipping on the rotten fruit.... I must be mad.

Brother Housen had finished his prayer, and it didn't occur to him that I might not want to pray after him. Yet I was full of outright rebellion, and I couldn't pray in the way he expected me to any more. The words would have choked me.

'God, what is this?' I began, not even closing my eyes, so God could see I was looking at the dump we were in. 'We've done everything you ask us to do. We've prayed in faith, we've proclaimed your truth. We've really done our bit. The only one who doesn't seem to be pitching in round here is you! Why don't you help us? Why don't you do it?' I couldn't round off a prayer like that with any grace, so I just said 'Amen'. Brother Housen obviously couldn't bring himself to add his 'Amen' to my little offering, because he came out with 'Thank you, Lord'. What on earth was he feeling thankful for now?

I couldn't quite meet his eyes, and as I glanced away a beaten up old car passed on the road. In the rear window a little sticker, just visible under the dust, proclaimed 'GOD IS ABLE'.

In silence, I pointed it out to him, and a big white smile split his face. As the car disappeared, I said it out loud: 'God is able.' Maybe God was letting us get to the end of our own strength and enthusiasm. I suddenly felt a great, unshakeable certainty well up in me, as though God were saying, 'OK, my children, now I'll show you what *I* can do.' I knew that God really could change lives, answer prayer, give me more pleasure than picnics on the beach.

'Let's give it another go,' I suggested. Brother Housen hugged me, and off we went.

A couple of minutes later I spoke to a bored young man sitting on a rickety fence. I explained the four spiritual laws as he sat there with his mouth open and his eyes gradually coming alive. When I finished he was very quiet.

'Well?' I asked.

'That's just what I want,' he said. Now it was my turn to open my mouth.

'What? Are you sure?'

'Yes, I'm sure.'

'But do you realise you must receive Christ and your life must change?'

'That's just what I want. I can't think of anything more wonderful.'

So I prayed a prayer, which he repeated after me, and I took his address, and gave him another tract. The angels rejoiced, and Brother Housen and I joined in.

We hadn't done anything different. We hadn't said anything new. Our feelings hadn't changed. Just from that moment, God stepped in. We talked to another group of four people, and as we spoke others crowded round to listen. By the time the market packed up for the day, four people had received Christ. We were in the clouds. God had moved in on the other side of perseverance and failure. When I feel failure now, I remember back to that lesson, that in failure I need to keep my eyes open, go on relating to God right in the middle of the failure so that I can learn something from it. If I give up too soon, if I decide that my gifts don't lie in this direction, or this is not God's will, then I am by-passing an opportunity to build my faith muscles.

That day was the start of something quite new. From then on, every time we went out to preach, it seemed that God gave us fruit. By the end of that year, sixty people, mostly youngsters, had given their lives to Christ and been baptised.

At school, and amongst my friends, I still had to live with embarrassed rejection and failure, feeling the terrible stigma of being a Christian in that society. The whites scorned me, no doubt due to my insecure, unloving attitudes towards them, and many of the blacks, who thought the Pentecostals were weird anyway, were just as dismissive of my efforts.

Yet now, by hanging on to my faith, even through failure, I began to see God move.

One day the pastor, Brother Howes, came to me and said, 'Brother Cooper, next time we go out in the open air, it's your turn to preach.'

'But I'm not ready yet! I don't know what to do!'

'Brother,' he said, clapping me on the shoulder, 'you just pray a lot about it. You'll be just fine.'

There was no way out of it. I had one week to prepare.

Man, I sweated! I cried out to God, I fasted even more than usual that week, but I couldn't get a clue of what God wanted to say. I wasn't guided to a theme, or any particular Bible passage, except the bit in Acts 2 where it says about young men and women prophesying, but it didn't fit in with anything else. I didn't know what to say about it at all, let alone make a whole sermon out of it.

Finally, the big day came. We had prayed that morning with great expectation, and the prayer meeting had been full of life, with many prophesies and many testifying to great blessing, but I still had no idea what I was going to say. I trembled as I put on my best suit and was bundled off in a big van with the others to a part of the island I had never seen before. As we scrambled out of the van, I prepared a quite different speech.

'Look this is ridiculous. Anyone could preach better than I could. I simply can't do it.' Somehow, though, everything moved too fast for me to be able to deliver even that statement. Suddenly, I was handed a mike. I took one step forward and began to preach the first sermon of my life.

I thought it would probably be my last. As I started, some of the little group drifted away, but a few stayed, and I kept going for them. Then as I went on, I lost track of time. I've no idea now what I preached, but from that first time I sensed the glory of preaching God's word. I was so blessed. As far as I know no-one was converted, but I felt like a lion.

Some time later I was invited to prepare two messages, one for young people on holiness. This time, God gave me something to say in advance, and I had a day I will never forget. As I spoke, God moved in such power by his Holy Spirit that I could see him touching those youngsters, and when I finished they came forward weeping to give their lives to Christ and to learn how to serve him. That evening we went out to preach in the open air. The whole village seemed to come out, as if drawn irresistably. As I spoke I sensed God like a great giant behind my words, speaking directly to hungry souls. Just seeing those people, held there by the Word of God, gave me a passion for evangelism that has never left me. I may be quite depressed when I start preaching in the open air, but the sight of even one person listening, the knowledge that they have a need of God even if they don't acknowledge it, overcomes any embarrassment or fear of ridicule. From those very first occasions I knew this was what my life was about. It is so hard to convey the glory, the sense of power flowing through you as you preach, and the wonderful satisfaction of seeing precious souls won to God.

As he listened that day, one man realised he was very, very thirsty, and rushed back home for a glass of water. He drank it as he listened, and then went back for another glass. When he returned with his third glass of water, he heard me say the words of Jesus, 'If any man thirst, let him come to me and drink...'. Then he knew that his thirst was a spiritual thirst, and he decided to come to Christ for the living water. He was just one of many convinced of their need for salvation that evening.

As Brother Howes hugged me goodnight, his face was tired but radiant. 'Dear brother, a day to remember, eh?'

I discovered that day that God's work is done through God's anointing. God is not forced into action because you are clever, because you have the right words, or the training. I owe to the Pentecostals that awareness of the need for seeking God, calling down his power, his strength and his glory. I learned to listen to the Spirit, and look entirely to him for success in God's work.

But alongside the wonder of seeing God move as the year progressed, there was also the pain of seeing that my lifestyle drove away from Christ the very people I was trying to reach. I got so frustrated and upset.

One day after yet another fruitless conversation with one of the teachers, I turned off the road home into a bar. I was particularly aware of my failure as an evangelist, and having asked for a glass of iced water, slumped at the bar, angry at God. I was still carrying a Bible, and felt that God wanted me to talk to the barman, who was using the lull in business to dry a few glasses.

'God,' I snapped, 'If you want to speak to that man you'll have to do it with your own Word. Anything I say is useless. So I'll do no more than read him the Bible. You'll have to use that from now on, as obviously you don't want to use any words I have found so far.'

So I read the whole of John chapter three at the poor man as he wiped down the bar and dried the glasses, and then I got up and went outside. 'That's that, Lord. All I can manage. Over to you.'

A few minutes later a bar-maid came out to find me.

'What on earth have you done to him?' she asked. 'He's in there blubbering like a baby.' Sure enough. The fellow was weeping uncontrollably.

So I rushed back in and heard how his mother was a Christian, but he had backslidden, and how God had touched him again. It was a powerful lesson. God acts when he wants to act, and if I want to see people come to Christ I need to rely on the promptings of the Spirit, and fill my message with God's Word.

From the moment of my conversion I knew I wanted to work for Jesus. I read *The Cross and the Switchblade*, and thought I would work in New York. Then I read Arthur Blessit and switched to Los Angeles. Then I wondered whether a linguist wouldn't be better used as a Bible translator in Deepest Africa. As the academic year came to a close, I really didn't know whether God wanted me to stay on Montserrat, since I was learning so much, or whether I could face another year of the school. Although I was conscientious, my teaching career wasn't a great success.

Another big failure was my attempt to run the Christian Union in the school. It was quite a big group when I took it over, but they seemed to spend all their time playing games, and when I started some serious Bible study they showed themselves as fairly nominal Christians. This just wasn't good enough. I started a full-blown Christian doctrine course–and they thinned themselves out until just a few children of Pentecostals were left. The others all disappeared, and eventually I closed down the group. What a defeat! I couldn't understand why these failures occurred, despite all that prayer. I was only just learning the dynamics of building God's church, the battle and the toil it involves.

I did get one opportunity to impress my sceptical friends, though. One night I was walking home from a prayer meeting with a Pentecostal friend when I became aware of someone hanging around in the shadows. He seemed drawn to us, and walked along beside me. In my spirit an unease stirred: I sensed something was wrong. I began to pray in tongues quietly.

As I did so, he began to rant and rave, mocking and blaspheming, and when I looked at him in the light of a window we were passing I could see a real demonic presence in his eyes. I began to speak in tongues out loud, and he became even wilder, shouting me down with horrible insinuations about church people and executing weird little dancing steps with arms flapping. It was obviously the demon taking control. By this time we were quite near my house, and I could see he wasn't going to leave us alone.

'In the name of Jesus Christ, I command you to come out of this man, you tormenting spirit!' I had to shout to make myself heard above his babbling. He convulsed as a spirit left him, and then began leering and writhing in quite a different manner. I cast out three spirits by name as my friend prayed beside me. I knew there were more, but the man begged me to stop. By this time he was slumped on the ground, and as I bent down to speak more gently to him, I caught sight of four of my VSO friends, staring with horrified fascination at us through a bedroom window. Summoned by the shouting, they were transfixed at the sight of me dispatching demons, and who could blame them?

Now that the man was more rational, I heard his sad story of sliding from faith into drunkenness. My Pentecostal friend and I prayed for him, but I knew he had been delivered against his will, and was not surprised when I heard later that he had returned to his old ways.

Returning home, I found myself in the role of hero among my VSO friends. They had been quite frightened by what they had seen, so in an attempt to reassure them I told them about other spirits I had dealt with, gave them guidelines to recognise what they were dealing with, and told them that only Christ has the power to overcome evil and protect them. For a while after that they treated me with real respect.

But I still didn't know what to do about the future.

Then one Sunday, a Pentecostal missionary came through and took a missionary service.

'Jesus sent us out into the world to make disciples,' he thundered. Yes, I nodded. 'He sends us out into a world of tremendous need.' I agreed. 'We should be willing to give up everything and go where he leads us.' Fine. I'd already reached this point in my thinking. It was a fine exposition, but nothing new to me.

The preacher closed in prayer and announced a hymn number. As I began to sing, I suddenly found tears rolling down my face. Brother Howes, who had an instinct for the way God works, pointed to me and said, 'Brother Cooper, will you give the closing prayer?'

And as I prayed, the power of God came upon me in great force. I saw the millions of souls without Christ, standing in endless untidy ranks, ashamed, silent, dark with fear and doubt, bound in the direction of even greater darkness. Then I saw the power of the Gospel to release them, and I was filled with a deep longing to preach Christ to them. It all poured out of me as I prayed. I shouted. I ended up at the front of the church, with everybody praying for me and prophesying. When the bewilderment and the sense of glory had passed I was clear about one thing: God had confirmed that he had called me, and wanted to use me as an evangelist. This was not a radical change of direction for me, but I always think of that evening when people ask how I knew what God wanted me to do.

Although I had no clearer idea of the future, I felt some action would be appropriate, so I wrote a few letters, including one to All Nations Christians College as the Wycliffe Bible Translators had suggested. Much to my surprise I got a letter of acceptance just a few weeks later—no interview, no further complications. Except money. I had none stashed away to cover the fees. Without much hope I wrote off to Surrey County Council who had given me a grant for University, and they gave me another grant.

This sort of guidance was a lot less dramatic than the storm and weeping which accompanied my 'call', but it was just as effective. I was really encouraged. The future seemed to be opening up, and God going before me. I was thrilled.

Perhaps because I was more relaxed about things, the rest of my stay on Montserrat became more and more pleasant. The children didn't do as well in their exams as I had hoped, but they were good to me and seemed to like me. Some of the staff looked almost wistful when I said I was leaving.

One day, the female half of the adulterous couple I had unwittingly denounced, who was not surprisingly one of my most whole-hearted denigrators, took me on one side and said, 'Alf, I'm going to hell. Pray for me.' For a moment I thought she was taking the mickey again, until I looked at her. Tears were in her eyes, and all her self-confidence had dissolved, leaving her so sad and empty. She knew that she needed Christ. Something of what I had been saying had got through after all. No matter how much people pretend not to need the Gospel, behind the mask of complacency and self-sufficiency there is inside a hunger for God, and this is the evangelist's greatest ally.

Yet I was still not above making a fool of myself. I took everything so seriously.

I had been wearing glasses for short-sightedness all my school life, and when my personal appearance began to matter at thirteen, my mother had bought me contact lenses. Sometimes I wore them, sometimes the glasses. Now I felt that wearing contact lenses was sheer vanity, so I threw them away and wore glasses all the time, to make myself as ugly as possible. Of course, people who suddenly saw me in glasses commented that they didn't know I was short-sighted.

'Ah,' I thought, 'perhaps God is telling me that I need to ask for healing of my sight.' The rather naïve faith of the Pentecostals, which so released God's power in some situations, brought me to the point where I really believed this. I read a magazine article by Oral Roberts, which said that I could lay my hand on the magazine and claim my healing. The great day came: it had to be a clean break, so I tossed my glasses into the rubbish bin, screwed up every last ounce of faith and prayed. I just knew that my eyes were going to get better. Indeed they were for a day or so, until they got tired, then I was as blind as a bat.

I spent the last month of my time in Montserrat blinking around in a fuzzy world. God was good to me: I was able to recognise my friends, and write the end of year reports without too much headache, so that few people knew what I had done. I left a misty Montserrat in a blurred aeroplane and was met by a hazy crowd of people from which my family eventually detached themselves and came into focus.

It was wonderful to see them again, although there was quite a bit of reverse culture-shock as I found myself in Rickmansworth where they had come to live from Chile. I couldn't fool them for long. Over tea, the whole story of the glasses and lenses came out. I told them, like the good Bible-college student I was about to be, that I believed that God was going to heal me.

They were all Jehovah's Witnesses, as they had been ever since my mother's 'conversion' to the sect soon after I left Chile for school in England. I thought people who could swallow those doctrines would have no trouble encompassing my situation, but as I watched their reaction, albeit through 'a glass darkly', I knew their opinion of me was confirmed.

They loved me, as I loved them. It was just a pity that I was quite round the bend.

# CHAPTER FIVE

# WHO NEEDS BIBLE COLLEGE?

All Nations Christian College is a beautiful country house surrounded by acres of woodland, particularly striking at the start of the academic year when the trees are beginning to turn to gold and the cock pheasants scuttle off startled into the ferns. Not that I saw much of it, of course. The confusion of meeting a hundred new people from all corners of the earth was compounded by my poor sight. I peered my way around the academic block until I found the name 'Martin Goldsmith' on a door—my tutor. I had met him in the early morning worship group, but this was my individual 'How to get the best out of your time here' interview.

A Jewish Christian, thin as a lathe, with one of the most expressive faces and bodies I have ever seen, Martin Goldsmith is above all a very quick man. He moves quickly, talks quickly and thinks even more quickly. After an enquiry about my general well-being, he flipped through my application form on the desk in front of him.

'Obviously you're not going to have any problems on

the academic side: you have a good university education and a good mind. But you've also done a lot of first-
hand ministry, especially evangelism. What do you
think you're going to learn here that you don't know
already?'

I looked at his quizzical smile. Was he pulling my
leg? How could he know that in my heart of hearts I felt
that the anointing of God was all I really needed?

'I'm here because God sent me here, and because I
need a deeper knowledge of the Bible and some time to
find out where he wants me to be.' All that was true, at
least.

'But you think a year locked away in a Bible School
is quite enough, don't you?'

'I know there's a lot for me to learn.' It was uncom-
fortable having my own thoughts spoken aloud by
someone else.

'There's a lot more than head knowledge gets learnt
here, you know. However, let's have a look at the
timetable choices and work out the most suitable
options for you. You'll need all the biblical stuff, Biblical Basis of Mission, Communications, Pastoral Counselling. Might as well do Greek, since you're a linguist.
You'll find the various Church History courses surprisingly useful. Here's a separate sheet with the
choices for practical courses, but you don't need to
decide about those just yet. Do you have some problem
with your sight?' he broke off as he saw me holding the
green sheet of paper at the end of my nose.

Meekly, I told him what had happened. 'I don't
think I believe God is going to heal me any more,' I
concluded. 'But what does it all mean?'

'It means you have learnt the hard way that you

can't buy your healing with faith. You can't force God to heal you.'

'I know that really, but I thought he wanted to heal me. I realise I was wrong. But what do I do now?'

'Go and see an optician?' he suggested with eyebrows raised quizzically.

So I did, and ordered both specs and lenses. In due course they arrived, and of course a hefty bill with them. And then God showed me his love in an extraordinary way. The very next day I got a cheque in the post which covered the amount exactly: no-one could possibly have known the amount or the timing of my need. This was just the loving touch from God I needed. He knew what I had been going through, and now he was supplying my healing in a much more orthodox manner. There is a place for faith, and for prayer, but only God can heal. I have seen many miracles of healing since then, but I am still short-sighted.

Now I could really get on with some work, and I found the lectures and seminars not only mentally stimulating, but spiritually uplifting. It was wonderful to get to know the Bible through and through, hearing it so beautifully taught and expounded, and learning to apply it. Then there was the thrill of mission and the discovery that over and above the emotion which swept through me at the thought of introducing others to Jesus was a whole field of study to be explored. How did God's plan for mission unfold in the Bible? What part does the Holy Spirit play in convincing an unbeliever of their sin? What mistakes have been made in the history of mission which we can learn from? What guidelines can we deduce from the Bible about spiritual warfare? How can you encourage church growth? We studied mission from all angles, and the coming together of the pieces was glorious. It excited me, swelled up in my heart like a fire...and then left me frustrated, because it was all theory, theory, theory.

'Is this really the best way to train for God's work?' I fumed at my tutor Martin. 'I just want to go and get on with it.'

'Next term you'll do some practical evangelism in Harlow,' he said soothingly. 'And you have your weekly church placement.'

'But do I need all this theory? I've heard the word of God preached with great power by men who had trouble reading the text they were expounding, men who wouldn't have a clue about the theories of dating the synoptic gospels, or about the christological debate.'

'Most of us on the staff here have been missionaries. We know you can't force God to work by writing brilliant essays. The people who come here to study come as tools who have placed themselves at God's service. If they weren't in God's hand, they wouldn't be any good. But there is some value too in sharpening up those tools, honing and perfecting them. That is what we are doing. Just ask God to show you where you need a bit of polishing.'

In some ways, my inner debate about what made a good missionary went on, and I still believe there is value in further education for Christian leaders. Some need it, but a great many more have it for the wrong reasons, because the church is based on the wrong assumption that a leader must necessarily be an academic. Yet after about a term, I could see that this was a once-in-a-lifetime opportunity to get some studying behind me, and I decided to stay on for a second year. I never shook off the frustration of wanting to get on with God's work, but those two years were the most peaceful and in some ways enjoyable of my life, and I will always be grateful for all I received there.

One of the great riches was to live and work with Christians from other parts of the world, from other denominations. I considered myself at that time to be a house-churchy, charismatic type, and had little time for any one denomination. I saw that each one was built around one specific aspect of God's revelation, some truth that was precious to a particular group of people, and this had crystallised into a structure. Some denominations had chosen a more central truth than others, some had remained flexible while others had become very hide-bound. This mattered little to me. I just felt I could have fellowship with anybody who knew and loved Jesus.

The mix of cultures was no problem for me: quite the reverse. A childhood in Chile and the last year in the Caribbean made me a cultural mix in myself. My great friend and room-mate, Samuel del Coso, and I formed a latin duet of prayer, arriving late for meals and serenading the lady-tutors in the late evenings. We had fun! Yet I still found some difficulty in relating to the other students.

Seeing me pack up my reading notes in the library one cold afternoon, Hans looked at his watch and closed his book as well. Following me out, but mindful of those still working, he waited until the door had sealed them into their studious silence.

'I've had enough virtue and hard work today, Alf. How about a game of table tennis?'

'I'm tempted,' I said back over my shoulder as we came down the stairs, 'but I don't think I will. I've got a prayer meeting for China at five.'

'Exactly so,' he agreed, taking the door I was holding open for him. 'What are you doing for the next hour?'

'Preparing for it.'

'But I thought Zak was leading this week. I saw him looking for a map yesterday.'

'Oh, I'm not leading. I just need to pray myself into it.'

'You pray to prepare for a prayer meeting? Really, Alf, you are too much. I shall just have to go and find some very unspiritual girl to play table tennis with. Not many of them are good at it, but they say if you want a wife to go overseas with, this is your last chance to look around. Good that there are many more women than men here, isn't it?'

'I'm not looking around for a wife. I'm looking up. God will tell me when I meet the right one. But have a good time, Hans. See you later.'

There was never any outright friction over all the disciplines I continued from my time in Montserrat— the fasting and the praying—but I often came up against incomprehension and irritation. One or two people confessed to me that they felt condemned by me, and perhaps I came across as arrogant and super-spiritual. I really wasn't trying to prove anything, and just expressed the way I saw life, but they found this hard to swallow. My spiritual armour was a bit too intact.

Of course, there were lots of girls around, and many of them I appreciated on a spiritual level. Some I even 'tried for size' in my mind, as it were. But this only ever led to confusion, so I kept them all firmly at arm's length emotionally. I had forgotten who suggested this tactic, but knowing my weaknesses it made sense to me, and I stuck to it, rather rigidly I suspect. I still teach it to any young people who will listen. I wasn't going to get involved until I was prepared to really commit myself.

I had a few lessons to learn in humility.

There was so much going on at college, all the time. I revelled in it. By the second year I was secretary of the student body and evangelistic rep on top of a heavy lecture schedule, the normal round of prayer meetings and worship groups which I wouldn't dream of missing, and the maintenance work which kept the college fees so low. Then I agreed to put on a play for an evening entertainment.

Suddenly one afternoon all these jobs seemed to scream at me together, and I knew I was sinking. I couldn't stand it any more. I couldn't face looking for one more person in the lunch queue, or finding urgent notes in my pigeon-hole. I escaped into the woods in despair.

'God, I just can't do all these things. I think I'm cracking up. You've got to help me.'

As I blundered on down the path, kicking at stones in my frustration, it seemed to me that God showed me an In Tray and an Out Tray. Then he said, 'Look, you can't do these things because you are trying to do them in your own strength. Now why don't you stop being so anxious and put them, one by one, into my In Tray and leave them there. Every responsibility and job, every message and errand that is weighing so heavily upon you, give them to me. Then stop worrying and go about your business. You will find that one by one they will appear in my Out Tray.'

So then and there I went through the whole lot, looking at each one individually and then committing it to God's In Tray and leaving it there. It took quite a long time, but it left me with a tremendous sense of peace. I walked back to college, and immediately began to experience miracles of organisation.

I'd go looking for someone, and find that they were having coffee in their room with two or three other people I also needed to see—married people who should have been at home and out of college for the afternoon. In five minutes I could get through work that I thought would take hours. People would ask me to swop places on a rota, and I would realise that the pressure was suddenly transferred to a day when I had more time. It was fantastic how the load dropped off my back.

God was showing me that his economy of time works in quite a different way from ours. We get our values and priorities all mixed up, but it is wonderful, if we will only put things in his In Tray, to see them appear, in his own timing, in his Out Tray. Everything that God wants us to get done will get done, whether family commitments, practical responsibilities or high-profile jobs like preparing and preaching a sermon.

This doesn't mean that I don't get flustered from time to time, but I let that panic now be the trigger for the image of God's In Tray, and it comes back to me again and again. When pressure comes I can get angry, frustrated and anxious, and start taking it out on other people: sometimes things turn up in my own Out Tray by this method, but I usually end up hating myself. Or I can go through the same sort of pressure and actually enjoy it, because of the pleasure of seeing how God is going to deal with this load.

All in all, I did a lot of maturing at college. I learned how to relate better to other people, and to decide what knowledge was going to be useful and how to absorb it. Above all, getting to know the Scriptures in depth was a privilege and a joy. I began to see the books of the Bible as a vast library, and learned where I could pick out just the passage, or the theme that I needed. This to me was the great advantage of having been to theological college. Not just what you learn there, but that you learn how to learn from God's word, and you know where to look, so your knowledge can go on expanding and deepening as you need it. I still believe that true training is done on the job, and was very excited by the concept of Theological Education by Extension which I learned about at college. This is a system used widely in Latin America to train up church leaders without ever taking them away from their work situation. It seemed absolutely right to me. Little did I know just how close I was later going to get to that school of thought!

I learned, on a personal level, the value of deeper learning when my sister, who was a Jehovah's Witness, turned up at College with her boyfriend from Spain. Rejected by my family on the basis of her sinful relationship, they had arrived desperate at College. She testifies to this day that she found Christ there, through the love shown them and the fact that here people obviously studied at as great, if not greater, a depth as the Jehovah's Witnesses. It was important to her that we knew what we were talking about.

From Day One I had stated my desire to find out what God wanted me to do, and as the terms flashed by this became an increasingly urgent need. Through thinking about mission so much, and getting to know myself much better, two convictions emerged. Firstly, Bible translation work wasn't for me. I needed to be where the people were, feeling their hunger and feeding them. Secondly, I was not an 'isolated tribe in the jungle' man. I needed a big city, with bustling crowds and potential for growth of big churches. So I went back to my original surmise about working with drug addicts, probably in the States.

Many missionaries passed through the college to tell us about their work. Colin Grant was the head of the Evangelical Union of South America, and though unspectacular in what he said, he not only gave us some solid teaching, but held our interest—not an easy feat in the fourth lecture of the morning while our thoughts were wandering towards the dinner queue. At the end of lecture, Martin Goldsmith realised he needed to be in two places at once, and caught my eye.

'Colin, this is Alf Cooper, who grew up in Chile. He'll show you where to find the dining room, and I'll meet you there. Thanks, Alf.' Martin shot off.

'When did you leave Chile, Alf?' Colin and I joined the end of the noisy queue.

'Oh, ages ago. I've got very little contact there now.'

'But you are going back, aren't you?'

I was struck dumb, but he could see it was a new thought.

'Well, it seems obvious to me, but then I've got South America on the brain. Do you speak Spanish?'

'Yes,' I stammered. 'I've got a degree.'

'Well, what do you think you are going to do with it?'

'Use it among the Hispanics in New York.' It sounded like a robot speaking, and I heard the life drain out of the idea as I said it.

'I'd hate to side-track you, but...' Colin hesitated. I cut in.

'No, you're right. I can't believe I'd never thought of it before.'

My Pentecostal experiences had led me to expect big flashes of light, prophecies, and weeping on my knees for God to show me where to go. Now, perhaps because I was in England, I needed to learn a different way, and I'm glad that I did. This is the way of working out, with common sense and prayer, which doors are opening and which you should go through. As you move forward, so God confirms with an inner peace that you are doing the right thing. I needed the peace, because I had a few surprises coming round the bend.

Apart from the Evangelical Union of South America that Colin Grant worked for, the other obvious agency was the South American Missionary Society. Martin had a lot of contact with SAMS, so I had heard about it, but after all it was an Anglican outfit. How could Anglicanism fit into Latin America?

A few weeks later, a friend invited me to a meeting where a bishop from South America was speaking. As David Pytches talked about his work I sensed a rightness about the man. I saw that God had made this Englishman into a Chilean in some deep area of his being. The Holy Spirit had worked to produce a wholeness and a naturalness about him. There was no great flash of insight, but I began to put flesh on the idea of Anglican work in South America.

I heard at that meeting that there was to be a valedictory service for the Pytches later that month in London. As a test I took along my friend, Samuel del Coso. He was very much a house-church type, who had recently come into the fulness and gifts of the Spirit. He had done some hospital visiting, and prayed with people who had been healed. I felt I could really test the authenticity of my feelings with him. He wouldn't be interested in any denominational mission, least of all Anglican.

'Surely this isn't Anglican!' You could see the surprise on his face after only ten minutes of the service. The liturgy was there, but so was the love, and the joy, and the openness to the Spirit that was to us the heart of worship.

'Yes,' he said after a few more minutes, 'this is right.' And it was.

Never had SAMS received a letter from a less likely candidate, or so I thought.

'I'm not an Anglican, and have no intention of becoming one,' I wrote. 'I don't expect to stay with you for long, but I believe God has guided me to you, perhaps to find me a teaching job...'

They obviously had to see this cheeky upstart for themselves, and invited me to their orientation course. At every step along the way was this sense of rightness. Every now and again there would be a stab of doubt—after all I hadn't chosen either South America or the Anglicans for myself—but as the questions arose and found answers, and the hurdles appeared and were overcome, I knew this was right. After All Nations I was going to Chile with SAMS.

There was a gap of a few months between the two, however. My family had moved to Cornwall, so I went back there to prepare. Despite my prayers, they were still convinced Jehovah's Witnesses, and I wanted to talk to them about it all again.

In vain. I tried not to antagonise them, but every discussion ended in argument. I cried out to God, and he gave me five words: 'Compassion, kindness, lowliness, meekness, patience.' That was what I was to concentrate on, and leave him to do the convincing and the convicting. From then on, we just had a lovely time together.

I had a lot of reading to do about Chile. The military *coup* of 1973 when Allende had been overthrown by Pinochet had filled the newspapers with conflicting reports. Was it a land of tanks and blood in the streets, or a land of peace and prosperity? I needed to know.

On a more practical level, there were a few items of equipment I decided I needed, and I didn't have enough money. I put the list before God, and asked him to provide.

In Mexico once, when I had nothing to eat, I had walked into a restaurant with no money, sat down and said grace. To my amazement a black car-park attendant had walked in at that moment and put money on my table. After my 'black angel' experience I never doubted God's ability to provide again. Rather unwisely I told my mother I knew God would provide for my needs, and reminded her of this story.

'You'd better not let Tom hear you talking like that,' she said. 'He's already asking me when you're going to stop swanning around living off other people and do a decent day's work.'

Put like that, I could see my step-father had a point. A self-made man, Tom was a hard worker, and I respected him for that. I must have looked like a real drifter to him, and because I valued our open and friendly relationship, I longed to show him that I was not avoiding work. I told him I was going out to look for a job.

'You'll be lucky, Alfred. There's not much around here. I'll come down to the labour exchange with you, though: I need a new blade for my hacksaw.'

There was nothing. He sympathised with me as he saw the reality of the situation dawn on my face. We walked hom in silence, until I said, 'You know, God is going to get me a really good job.'

Back to silence.

The next day I was walking through St Austell, and God nudged me into the Post Office. I made enquiries, and found there was a job going in Par, where I was living. I signed up and went home a postie! Tom had the grace to be thrilled for me. It meant getting up at five o'clock, which is probably why it hadn't been snatched up before, but by half past nine it was all over and I had all the day to study. Perfect! I worked at this until just before I left, and made enough money to pay some housekeeping and buy every last item on my list.

Amazingly, my family had chosen to move from Rickmansworth, where I had the support of St Andrew's, Chorleywood, to Par, where I joined a Pentecostal Church under Don Double, one of the men who has taught me most about faith and ministry. Over the years he has taught me about ministering to people in the power of the Spirit, stretching my expectations and training me thoroughly, but in such a humble way that he has become a friend at the same time. Later in Chile he came out to visit me and to lead campaigns, for which I interpreted. I am so grateful to him and to God, who used my unbelieving family to guide me to two churches which have both played such a vital part in my spiritual life.

My post round covered the little village of St Blazey, and about half way through the round I passed the Anglican church of St Blaise, a large church, dusty and musty, smelling of death and incense. I got in the habit of stopping there to catch my breath and pray a little. I asked God to help the church, but it didn't seem very likely, so I prayed much more for myself, and carried on.

One morning, the Vicar caught me coming out of his church. He was intrigued, having never met a praying postman, especially at seven o'clock in the morning. When I gave my credentials as a missionary going to South America, he said he'd love to talk to me, because he'd been reading about Liberation Theology. This movement, which had started in the Catholic church in South America, was an important part of the theological landscape there, and its influence was spreading fast. I had 'done' Liberation Theology at college in some depth. We agreed that I would go to see him on Thursday night.

I don't think we came to any conclusions about Liberation Theology, but we started to talk about ministry. Malcolm was a young Anglo-Catholic priest who had started out full of hope. A few years of a handful of unenthusiastic old ladies at St Blazey had really knocked the hope out of him.

'I feel as dead as the ash that I place on the people's foreheads on Ash Wednesday,' he admitted. 'I don't know if I can go on much longer.'

I found it difficult to believe we were serving the same God. Ministry with the Spirit is fantastically wonderful, but ministry without his power is worse than a waste of time, it is a dead weight, a negative force in the minister's life. Yet it didn't feel right to bounce in and bubble on about joy and power. I told him about some of my experiences of the Holy Spirit in fairly muted terms, but it didn't seem to pierce his gloom. I pleaded my early start in the morning and left. I must have prayed for him, because I pray systematically through the list of people I have contact with during the day, but it was a sad and sorry situation, and I put it out of my mind.

The following Monday morning, when I delivered his letters, I found a note pinned to his back door. I don't know what the milkman had made of it. It read, 'Hallelujah! God has baptised me with his Holy Spirit!'

'Poor man,' I thought. 'He's tried everything, now he's trying to use the right language.' As I trudged back down the path, I heard a rattling of bolts behind me, and then he came at me like a crow, flapping his black cassock and squawking incoherently. I was so surprised I dropped letters all over the place, and nearly ran away in fear before I realised he was trying to hug me.

At last he found some words, 'Alf, it's fantastic. I think I'm going to burst! God really does love me!'

I thanked God with a shout of laughter as I saw the radiant face and the new-found energy of the man.

'Malcolm, what happened?'

There, on the damp pavement, with the blank early-morning windows of the granite houses opposite as witness, he gave his testimony for the first time.

'When you left on Thursday, I felt so desperate. It nearly choked me. I went back to my study, banged my forehead on the bookshelf and cried, "God, give me this Holy Spirit." Nothing happened, and I went to bed.

'On Friday morning, at Matins, I had to preach from a passage from John 5, you know, about the paralysed man at the pool of Bethesda. As I read the passage aloud from the pulpit, I heard a voice saying, "Malcolm, do you want to be healed?"

'It sounded out loud, like a real person talking. I completely forgot about the tiny congregation and answered with a glad cry, "Yes".

'And then the Holy Spirit just poured all over me, and in me, until I was overflowing. I was drunk in the pulpit. My sermon was a torrent of praise. The liturgy was just another way of telling Jesus I loved him. I've been on a high ever since. I just want to go on worshipping Jesus for ever.'

It was wonderful to see him like this, and we arranged to meet again later in the week. He was just beginning to tell me that he had been given the gift of tongues in the meantime, when suddenly the piano behind him played a note. He turned white.

'Was that the cat?' I asked, a little naïvely.

'No, the cat's in the kitchen. That was the monk. He used to live here a hundred years ago. Every now and again he comes back. I see his ghost in the passage and he scares me silly by playing the piano at night.'

'Right, well that was his farewell concert,' I said briskly. 'We're going to send him packing.'

So we did, Malcolm performing his first exorcism in the power of the Spirit, thereby giving him a chance to demonstrate his new prayer language. The 'monk' never visited the Vicarage again.

As for Malcolm, he began to expound the Scriptures with new life, and to exalt Christ. He had encouraged a few parishioners into the gifts of the Spirit before I left for Chile. All this helped my growing realisation that God's Spirit is not hindered by structures—only by structured and hardened hearts. God responds powerfully when we sincerely open doors and windows to his Spirit. He can take the dustiest, deadest bones and breathe life into them.

When I went back to a service three years later there he was, preaching Jesus. It was still Anglo-Catholicism, the incense was still swinging, but the place was packed with converted people, and there was blessing, and healing, and great, great joy.

# CHAPTER SIX

# CHILE PARA CRISTO!

By the time I arrived in Chile, my thoughts were in turmoil.

In one sense I was going home. I had grown up there until the age of nine, and my sister, Granny and other relatives still lived there. Yet my memories of the Chile I loved had to be overlaid with the press reports of the takeover by Pinochet: streets swarming with tanks and rivers running with blood, ordinary people being snatched by night and disappearing for ever. It could be a pretty rough homecoming.

Not only Chile had changed. I was not the same person as when I left either. I was a Christian now, and that brought other aspects to my confusion. I had read that a massive 15% of the population were born-again, Hallelujah-shouting Pentecostals: when I lived there I hadn't met a single believer, to my knowledge. My heart leapt at the thought of worshipping in the Spirit as I had with the black Pentecostals on Montserrat, but with my own people, in the vibrant Latin American way. But Alf, stop! You can forget all that. You're going to be working with Anglicans. Anglicanism? How does the polite, apologetic, dusty little Anglican church relate in South America? It seemed absurd.

At least I had a job, and somewhere to stay. But why had God catapulted me across the world to serve him in such an unpromising situation? There was no way I could fit in with this Anglican set-up for long. Theologically and culturally we were surely mismatched. On the flight over I read an article in *Renewal* magazine about the renewal movement in the church in England. One leader, David Watson, said, 'Be renewed, and stay in your denominational churches however dead they seem.' Another, Arthur Wallis, wrote, 'Be renewed, and get out of the dead churches: start afresh in a house church.' I knew which idea excited me more. If I had stayed in England the established church wouldn't have seen me for dust. So why was I running into the arms of an Anglican bishop? God must have had a bad day in the guidance department.

Perhaps this job was just a springboard, and I would leap from there into an exciting, fulfilling, all-out ministry among the Pentecostals. Under all the confusion was excitement, and a passionate belief that God had a purpose, but there would have to be a lot sorted out before the way was clear.

Santiago airport, and there were David Pytches, my diocesan bishop, and Colin Bazeley, my team leader. I had only met David briefly in England, but he had played such a large part in my being in Chile that I was grateful to him for his welcome. Colin was a large and comforting man, with smiling blue eyes—a father figure, one who would understand. As I shouldered my way through the loud Chilean crowds towards them, I suddenly felt that everything was going to be all right.

Bathed in a wash of Spanish emotion, surrounded by hugging Latin Americans, and suddenly relieved and very tired, I wanted to hug them...but they were English, and my bosses, so I decided against it. Colin saw my hesitation, and wrapped his arms round me anyway.

I wasn't a very good guest as we drove through Santiago. I just sat beside Colin as he drove, drinking in the heat, the smells and the sounds of my childhood. My lovely Chile was still there: the bright colours, the street stalls, the dust and the smiles hiding so much grinding poverty. Colin negotiated the crazy traffic with ease and waited calmly until I was ready to talk.

'It's been a long time...' I started to explain. 'It's good to be back.'

'We always feel that, even after only six months in England. This is our home now.' I sighed. He understood.

'You've got a great start here, you know,' encouraged David. 'You know the language and love the people already.' Colin laughed.

'In fact, you're probably more at home than we are in Santiago. We only came up from the rural South a year or so ago.' He paused to allow a beat-up old car to execute a noisy and unsignalled U-turn. 'The traffic's rather slower among the Mapuches.' I smiled, recognising that this was a massive understatement.

'I'll just take you to the Whiteheads today. You can stay there for a couple of nights until you've met the team, and then we can sort out where you're going to live. There's no hurry about anything. Take your time, talk to people, find your feet, and then you can tell me what you think you would like to do, OK?'

'Fine.' This was the sort of leadership I could cope with!

Gordon and Beryl Whitehead obviously knew from first-hand experience what one needs after a flight across the world. A small but neat and cheerful bedroom was waiting, a shower and a light meal, even though it probably wasn't a time of day they would normally eat. Colin stayed for the snack, and filled me in a little on the team that was gathering there.

'You ask the average man in the pew what he thinks of when you say "mission in South America". He'll talk about either poor Indians in the jungles, or vast grotty shanty towns around the big cities,' said Colin. 'And those are the people who support SAMS and keep in touch. The rest have even less of an idea. I spent all my last furlough trying to convince people that there is a middle-class South America, living much as the middle classes in England, who need the gospel just as much as the shanty towns and the isolated tribes.' Gordon nodded.

'It's not so appealing to the mission supporter in some ways as providing medicines to the outback, or soup kitchens for the homeless in the cities. But in fact with the Pentecostals, who are growing enormously but exclusively in the working classes, the upper-middles are being left out. Yet they're the ones we have got to reach with the gospel if we stand any chance of bringing social reform to Latin America.'

'And you should see the need,' put in Beryl. 'Behind all these smart entrances with their burglar alarms you have marriages crumbling, wives of workaholics hitting the bottle, children growing up with no emotional security at all.... Of course, we haven't been here very long, but already I'm beginning to feel swamped with people's problems.'

'Well, that all makes sense to me,' I put in, laying down my fork. 'So what are you actually doing, and what resources have we got?' I felt a need to be systematic, so that I could apply all the church growth teaching from college.

'As far as resources go,' admitted Colin ruefully, 'we've got people and that's about it. There's Barbara and myself, these two here with their family have come recently across from Vina del Mar on the coast. Five of the team have been here a bit longer, working in the hospitals and so on: the Robinsons, the Jacklins and Thea Coates. Then there are Ray and Gill Smith who work in the Anglican Community Church, which has an English-speaking congregation, mostly business men, and Felicity Houghton doing a great job with University Christian Unions. That makes quite a scattered team, but I'll take you to a few meetings until you've met them all.'

'It's all very new, really.' Gordon's gift of enthusing people came into play. 'We're just gathering steam, and you've come in at a crucial point. We've all settled, and we're getting to know people, and feeling our feet. If it sounds as though we haven't got a strategy, that's because we haven't crashed in from England with a ready-made, identikit mission plan. We're starting small groups in our living-rooms for the time being. We're still tuning into the situation and to God. We follow individual hunches, and submit them to Colin and the group, and wait for a pattern to emerge. It's very exciting.'

I was beginning to catch his enthusiasm, but the bald facts weren't very clear in my mind.

'You mean you have no church buildings, no evangelistic campaigns and no regular worship with Chileans?'

'Nope.' Gordon grinned at my directness. 'We have an odd selection of very ordinary people, with very little money, and we're trying to convert a city of five million people. You've joined a bunch of lunatics here, Alf. But at least with you coming that makes the numbers up to twelve, and there's a good precedent for a team of twelve turning the world upside down.'

I had to admit, as I woke up luxuriously slowly ten hours later, that I liked these people, and what they were doing. Yes, they were crazy, in one sense. But they were crazy for God, and I could relate to that. I had also seen some of the back-up team they had in England, at SAMS headquarters. Again, it was rather a shoe-string operation, always just managing to make ends meet economically, but with a tremendous sense of family, and good grass-root prayer support in the churches. They had linked me to several congregations before I left England, and helped me find someone who would distribute a regular prayer letter to two hundred praying friends. I knew I wasn't on my own, and that was a good start, even though I expected to leave these Anglicans behind me before too long.

My 'two or three nights' with the Whiteheads got extended by mutual consent. Their loving home provided me with just the base I needed, and their sense of humour knocked me back to reality if I got too serious. They had two daughters, Marianne and Kirsten, who bounced on me and shared their lives with me.

Eighteen months later I was still there. The whole family were just so good at accepting me and loving me without suffocating me. I was allowed to be myself. I

had lived with the deadlines of college and the puzzled
tolerance of my family long enough to appreciate being
treated as a responsible person with my own agenda.

There were, in those first weeks, two main items on
that agenda: visiting my family—especially my sister
Liz and my granny—and getting in touch with the
Pentecostals.

It was quite an experience to make contact with
aunts and uncles and cousins I hadn't seen for years.
They had had a fairly negative impression of what sort
of person I was: I had moved from the excesses of
University days to the fanaticism of a wandering
preacher who seemed incapable of finding himself a job
in life. I hope I managed to dispel this myth, and
certainly there was much fun and laughter as we caught
up on family news. They, for the most part, were
respectable pillars of the English community, and it
was interesting to get their input on the political situation.

On the whole, they were supportive of what had
happened in Chile. There had obviously been a lot to
criticise in the violent way things had been done, and
there was a strong sense of outrage on behalf of the
political prisoners who had been tortured and killed.
Yet there seemed to be a concensus, among rich and
poor alike, that Chile could not have gone on much
longer as it was under the Marxist experiment. There
was still room for improvement, but there was at least a
more sound economic base and signs of hope for the
future. As I suspected, the press reports in England had
been manipulated and exaggerated. However, I could
also see the social cost of imposed capitalism: jobless
families, harsh 'pay or lump it' policies in education,
medicine and commerce. Then, too, my heart went out

to some, now ostracised, who had sincerely hoped to change society's ills. You could see the bitterness and disillusionment in their eyes. What could bring reconciliation to divided Chile?

My sister Liz was married to the son of Allende's best friend, so she was able to shed more light on the situation. Her husband was in the States and she was left in Chile with two little children, so she welcomed me all the more gladly. Yet she was, like most of my family, an ardent Jehovah's Witness. I felt I should try, just once, to have it out with her, but I met the all too familiar wall of indoctrination which I saw as brain washing. There was no way she was going to come out of her shell, and that caused me pain because I loved her so much, but I just had to accept the situation. How frustrating for an evangelist!

Together we went off to see Granny, who was a regular attender at the Anglican church and so had a fair idea of what SAMS was all about. In fact, she had been led to Christ by Doug Milmine, a SAMS bishop now in Paraguay. He had spent quite a lot of time at her house, and one day had picked up a photograph of my father which stood on the piano.

'That's my son, Brian,' she explained.

'But I was in a German prisoner-of-war camp with Brian,' exclaimed Doug. So they developed quite a friendship.

Granny had prayed for me a lot over the years, especially since my father had died, and I was much encouraged by her support during what turned out to be the last years of her life.

'If you want to meet the Pentecostals, you may as well start big,' advised Gordon. 'Go to Jotabeche.'

Jotabeche was at that time one of the largest

churches in the world. I saw their preachers invading the city centre on Saturday, and I joined the enormous crocodiles of witness as they wound their singing, clapping way to the services. I shared in the beauty and the storm of their worship, and heard the roar as many thousands of them prayed out loud at once. It was two years since my time with the Pentecostals on Montserrat, and it was wonderful to feel part of this vibrant community again.

I knew from my reading at college that it had all begun in 1909 with an English Methodist missionary called Hoover. With a few Chileans he began to ask God to pour out his Holy Spirit as at Pentecost. Quite unknown to him, other groups were praying the same prayer in Azusa Street, Los Angeles and in North India at the same time.

Hoover and his friends began to experience the gifts of the Spirit, and to be involved in healing, but also to get in trouble with both their church and their community. At one early meeting they believed God told them to go out and preach, so they stood outside a local bar and began to preach. The barman, having never seen such a thing before, was furious, and advanced on the preacher brandishing a bottle. Whose nerve was going to break? Amazingly, before he could throw the bottle, the barman crashed to the ground as the Spirit fell upon him and he was soundly converted. What more confirmation did they need? Their preaching became even more aggressive.

This really set the pattern for the new church. Much, much prayer was involved, listening to the Spirit and then obeying what they heard, with a very dynamic form of worship and constant enthusiastic evangelism. This pattern still controls them, and of course it tied in so remarkably with my own convictions. The original Pentecost, as it happened in Acts, was not just an experience of the outpouring of the Spirit and the glory of God for the sake of the disciples. It was first and foremost for mission and evangelism, so they could invade enemy territory and take it with power.

In those early days among the Chilean Pentecostals, there was a prophecy that one day the President of the nation would come to their services. This was patently ridiculous. They were a small group, ridiculed by everyone, spat on by passers-by, and on many occasions even stoned. The Catholic church was quick to mobilise opposition to the movement, and many Pentecostals suffered appallingly at the hands of the Catholics. To this day the Pentecostals consider the Roman church as the Great Beast and the Harlot and any other symbol of Satan they can find in Revelation.

Despite this opposition, the fervent preaching paid off in terms of large numbers coming to Christ and joining the new church. It was not only what they said that attracted people: it was common knowledge that if you had a problem the doctors could not cope with, or if you could not pay for a doctor, you went to the Pentecostals. Although you only went for the healing, you had to sit through powerful singing, and the exposition of the word of God first, and after that it only took the fact that you were healed to drive the message home.

Suddenly, in the 1930's, the growth became exponential. Unfortunately, such fervour was not compatible with tolerance, and churches split again and again. Usually this centred round a strong leader who took a point of doctrine and emphasised it to the point where he would walk off and take half the church with him. There are over 3,000 Pentecostal denominations and groups in Chile today. This splitting syndrome is a wonderful mechanism for growth: when I arrived in Chile in 1975 around 10% of Chile was Pentecostal, and today it is reckoned to be nearer 20%.

Although this movement was restricted to the working classes, the politicians couldn't deny that it was a powerful group, and the fight was on to harness these votes. So it was that President Allende, and later Pinochet himself, started to come annually to Jotabeche. The old prophecy had been fulfilled, and now the church is marching on to their battle cry *'Chile para Cristo'*, 'Chile for Christ!'

Their big weakness is their lack of Bible teaching. They are rather proud of the fact that none of their leaders go to Bible College. 'My seminary is the streets': this is a common defence of their position, and one which I felt much in common with until I had been to Bible College. They look down their noses at any training. 'The letter kills the Spirit' they say, so they discourage their people from pursuing theological or even further secular education. This means that the upcoming generation, who are much more academically trained than their parents, are finding that their pastors cannot answer their intellectual questions. This is a time bomb of which they seem unaware, but one which concerned me greatly.

In fact, this is what stopped me joining them. It was a hard decision, because in so many ways I was attracted to them. I loved the fact that it was now an indigenous movement, raised up by the Spirit of God and so completely in harmony with the Chilean national character. I loved their worship, their use of gifts in evangelism, and their fervour, but the shallowness of their teaching was abysmal. This was brought home to me when for some reason I was asked to give a message on marriage. Despite being a most unlikely candidate for the job, I looked up what I believed the Bible taught and gave them that. They had never heard anything systematic on a subject that was so practical. They lapped it up. Soon I was swamped with requests to do the same talk in other churches, despite my protests that I knew nothing about it.

The sheer size of the Pentecostal churches made a painful contrast with the Anglicans. There was a church in a district called Renca with which we were supposed to be helping, and Colin, in his first bishop-to-trainee talk, asked me to teach a course on evangelism to the youth group.

I was so keen to get going, and put all my college learning into practice, that this seemed a very small project, but I went at it like a bull at a gate. I began to study, to pray and to fast, and realised as I put the material together that this was what life was about. I was completely sold on evangelism. I built up a fantastic head of steam, and was rather flattened when I arrived for the first meeting. There were just three young lads, fairly keen, bless them, and wonderfully tolerant of my difficulties in trying to adjust my glowing vision to their three slightly grubby, definitely wary faces.

Yet however limited the scope of this project, it was at least something to do. For the most part, I felt I was just kicking my heels. What was I supposed to be doing here?

I began to really seek God. In the middle of the city was a hill called Santa Lucia, from which you could see the whole of Santiago. I got into the habit of going there every Wednesday to pray and fast for the city as it lay spread out before me. From that vantage point I could see very clearly that we needed to plant self-multiplying churches. Each one would start small, of course, but would be raised on principles which would motivate them towards planting daughter-churches from the very beginning. This meshed in very well with the Anglican strategy as it began to emerge and be forged in the light of experience.

The sector of town on which the Anglicans were concentrating their efforts was called the Barrio Alto. This was a middle-class area with a radius of three to five miles and about half a million people living in it. Gradually a vision emerged to plant ten churches there. This was very presumptious, since we so far had only one teeny little house group.

This slower, more solid approach, laying Anglican foundations, seemed to me at the time too unadventurous. I had much to learn about God's ways and timing: his work, in practice, often unfolds far more fruitfully in his own time than according to our rushed and limited visions. I couldn't see how God would work in any context other than Pentecostal zeal, fire, intercession and fasting.

I can't remember ever being impressed at a church service by the notices until I heard the Pentecostals at Jotabeche.

'Monday night, prayer meeting for the whole church. Tuesday night, men's prayer meeting for their evangelism on Saturday. Wednesday, prayer and fasting for the whole church. Friday, the ladies pray all afternoon. Saturday, meet for an early morning prayer meeting before the evangelism teams go out to the neighbouring towns. Sunday, meet early for prayer if you want to support the witness processions into church...' It's no coincidence that there are eighteen thousand people sitting there listening to those notices!

Within any one service, there would be three or four 'seasons of prayer', where people just get together in groups and pray out loud in a great roar of urgent prayer all over the building. The way they prayed, the amount they prayed, showed that they really believed that prayer changes things.

This seemed right to me. What other theology of prayer made any sense? If prayer isn't high on your agenda, what is your concept of God?

Of course, the Anglican team prayed quite a bit, individually and together. Yet I couldn't help missing the old Montserratian Pentecostal concept of storming the thresholds of Satan's territory, wrenching souls from his grasp in prayer so that when you began the evangelism, things could really happen. I knew from rugged first hand experience that this had been essential in Montserrat, and the Pentecostals had found it true here in Chile.

Young and raw, I often spoke out impetuously at our Team meetings. The wiser missionaries listened patiently and loved me loads. Was I really intended for this Anglican style of ministry? Doubts would come and go. What was I here for? What could I really contribute?

# CHAPTER SEVEN

# WHERE THE PATH
# PETERS OUT

As I pleaded with God to help me find my rightful place in his plan, things began to happen.

One night in Renca, I took my three faithful lads out to do a spot of door-to-door visiting. When we returned to the church to discuss our experiences, which were less than totally positive, and to pray, I found someone waiting for me.

He was a tiny little chap. He reminded me of a mosquito: stick thin and full of noise and enthusiasm. He launched at full tilt into his speech.

'You must be Alfredo, yes? I've longed to meet you ever since I heard about you how you are teaching these young ones and how you are so Pentecostal and so on fire it does my heart good to meet you so I can share with you what the Lord has told me because he has been so good and you must meet my wife and come and help us pray because there is so much to do...'

Eventually I managed to cut in.

'May I know your name?' He was off again.

'Oh, I am so sorry. My name is Enrique. Enrique

Lincoñir. I live in La Florida. I always seem to start in the middle and then you don't understand me. My wife, Merla, she always says, well, you see my hand here, how mangled it is, well when I was a child I got it stuck in a spaghetti machine, and my wife, Merla, she always says that my head got stuck in there as well. Sometimes I think she is right. But my heart is good now that I have found Jesus and I just want to tell everyone. I read that the Gospel will be proclaimed from the roof-tops, so I climbed up a drain-pipe and started shouting to everyone about Jesus, but Merla said I was mad, that it was a good thing to want to do, but that I needed some help. Then the Holy Spirit guided me to a man in my church who told me about you, so now I have found you.'

He beamed at his achievement. I was more puzzled than impressed. 'But what do you want me to do?' He looked at me, amazed.

'But isn't it clear? You must help me to start a church.'

Immediately I loved this funny little man, and it looked like the opening I had been praying for, but what on earth would Colin and the team say? With some trepidation I told Colin the next time I saw him.

'It's not in the Barrio Alto,' I pointed out to him. 'It's a very poor area in quite the wrong part of town. And Enrique and his wife sound like more of a liability than an asset.'

'But there must be something good about it, or you wouldn't have mentioned it,' Colin reasoned.

'Well, even if it doesn't make sense, I would like to go out there and see what can be done.'

'You just carry on, Alf. We're here to plant churches,

and we need all the openings we can get. You go off and have a go.'

The next Sunday, a typically beautiful Chilean day of sunshine and light breezes, found me rocketing across the city in a jammed bus. From the large modern glassy houses, beautifully kept gardens and leafy parks of the Barrio Alto we passed through streets of enormous blocks of flats and then out into the no-man's-land of the 'campamentos'. Here wooden shacks were crammed together with no gardens at all, only large tracts of dry dusty ground invariably used as football pitches. Soon we were within half a mile or so of the cross Enrique had put on my map, which was as close as the bus-route got. Then I was on my own.

I followed a track off to my right between houses of breeze block, stepping out quite purposely at first, but losing momentum as the path petered out, and the houses became more and more makeshift. Babies played in the mud quite oblivious to the stench and the flies which pestered them. Sanitation was unheard of here. Every five hundred metres or so was a waterpipe which served upwards of a hundred families. The shanty shacks were tiny and built out of any rubbish they could scavange. Corrugated iron predominated, eked out with wood and cardboard, and of course the windows were open holes, or covered by plastic bags. I thought of the chill of the winter nights, and couldn't believe what I was seeing.

Enrique had given me the name of a road, but there were no maps for these shanty areas, so I had to trust those who told me I was going in the right direction. Had I misunderstood Enrique's assertion that the church would be in his kitchen? It seemed odd when he said it, because I thought a living room would be more appropriate: now my unease stemmed from the fact that I couldn't even see anything that looked like a kitchen round here. Then suddenly, I came across some houses which were partly brick and seemed to have some plumbing.

The system here was that the government built a bathroom and kitchen out of brick, a tiny structure about three meters square. Around this, tacked on in the best way possible, were the other rooms, fabricated out of the corrugated iron, sides of packing cases and other materials won from the rubbish tips. Enrique was an electrician, and his wife Merla was a maid, so they were better placed than many of the Mapuche Indians who had drifted to the city looking for work. Not only did they have one of these government plots, but they hoped soon to get more bricks and make another 'real' room. Their hope and their joy in this poverty-stricken situation seemed unimaginable, and emphasised for me the relative unimportance of material possessions. I tried not to let my amazement show as Merla led me into the kitchen. She probably worked in a house much like the one I lived in, and knew where I had come from, but there was no jealousy, and no sense of inferiority, just a fellowship and sharing in the gospel.

By this time Alf, church-planter *extraordinaire*, had abandoned any expectations, and it was fine by me that no-one else turned up. The three of us sat in the tiny kitchen and prayed for the church which was to be born there. We carved out a niche for God's kingdom, driving back the forces of evil that would prevent this church happening, and I really felt by the time I made my way back across the shanty town that I had done a good morning's work—every bit as important as preaching an evangelistic sermon to a hundred people.

Next Sunday, Enrique hailed me as I got within earshot: we had three new members, and he was so excited. A young lad had thrown some sort of schizophrenic attack, and Enrique had prayed for him until he calmed down. His mother was so impressed at the improvement in his behaviour that she had agreed to come to this 'church' with her son and a younger daughter, who had Down's syndrome. The sermon I had made myself prepare, despite my doubt I would need it, was hastily simplified even further, and we taught them a song or two, and prayed with them. This was the basis of our congregation–my first experience of church planting.

Now I understood how the Pentecostals had been so successful in Chile. Their method of growth was prayer, prayer, prayer until the power was there to demonstrate that God had something to offer. I began to pray for people to be healed, and feverish babies would cool down, breathe more deeply and sleep the fever away. Next week, the mother would be there again, usually with more of the family.

The kitchen was soon outgrown, but there was a Pentecostal church not far away. They were in some sort of leadership crisis, and were happy to lend us their building of zinc roofing slabs and wooden panels. After a two-day mission with visiting preachers and conscientious follow-up of people contacted, sixteen people were converted with their families. Within three months this church, which seemed so ludicrous an idea to start with, had become a reality.

Another area which looked promising was the work of Ray and Gill Smith, members of the Anglican team who were working among the English community. They made contact with two Chilean youngsters called

Nicholas and Patricio, and started what was known as the Holanda group. I went along to help with a retreat where they were asking God how they could reach out into society. Here were charismatic, evangelistic Christians with a house-church sort of mentality that really suited me. They were thinking people as well, and with twenty or thirty people it really felt like a church.

Yet as I spent time with their leaders I noticed a pride, a conviction that 'God is only blessing through us'. And if God was blessing them, then they must be doing everything right, so they didn't respond well to any suggestions from the likes of me.

As my links with the group grew, so they drew closer and closer to a movement called 'Renovacion'. This just means 'renewal', so it sounded reasonable, but the whole network was into very rigid structures of authority, demanding absolute submission of the members to the leaders. I hadn't come across this before, but it felt all wrong. From feeling that I should give my all to these people, I changed to wanting to withdraw completely.

Now I was really on my own. I couldn't join up with Renovacion, and the only alternative were the dear Anglican missionaries in the Barrio Alto who were trying to build the kingdom of God with little or no experience of church planting behind them. What was God doing in Chile? How could I get where the real progress was?

I felt this needed a special meeting with Colin, with nothing else on the agenda.

Colin listened to my carefully-prepared speech as it disintegrated into an outpouring of frustration and confusion, and which just stopped short of being a resignation address.

'What do you want to do, Alf? Get on a plane? It's a big decision.'

I looked at this man, so sane, so level-headed. He hadn't been insulted by my attitude to his team ministry, he hadn't tried to steam-roller me into a decision. He trusted me. Suddenly, I knew what was needed: not a new answer, but one which was rooted in a new openness.

'I'll pray.'

For four days I fasted. I prayed and read the Bible, asking God to show me where I should be.

I had never fasted for more than a day or so, but Beryl and Gordon went away for a little holiday, and I thought this was a good opportunity. I don't know what I expected, but I knew from the past that God's power could be released through fasting. There were no flashing lights, no voices, but just a calm conviction that I was in the right place, that I was in his plan.

The day Gordon and Beryl returned, I received letters from two people whom I had consulted in my confusion. Both of them clearly said, 'Stay loose from Renovacion'. One of them was Don Double, who was a leading light of the charismatic movement in England, and it seemed all the more striking that he should warn me off a group that was outwardly very similar. The other was John Perry, one of the wisest and most loving men I have ever known, vicar of St Andrew's. God seemed to be saying 'Don't get pushed into anything yet.' Although nothing much had changed, I was at peace.

I told my friends at Holanda that they wouldn't be seeing so much of me in the future. As time went on, I watched with pain as the truth of the situation emerged. There were actually two rival Renovacion groups vying to swallow them up. Here I could see at first hand the very divisive element in Chilean church life. Balanced with the prayer and the glory there is competition, jealousy, sometimes even hatred among the leaders. It smoulders under the surface, hidden by the great blessing and potential of all the budding young Christians. Over the next ten years I would see the whole sordid circle of splits, leaders falling into immorality or financial fiddling and the church crashing, then a merger leading to another split. The initial signs that things were going wrong were already in evidence when I was there. Now I see the danger signals as soon as a group drifts from a Bible-based Christianity to an experience- and man-centred Christianity. While there is much we can learn from the Pentecostal patterns of worship and prayer, I came to appreciate the theological balance and consistency of the Anglican set-up. Today, I'm pleased to say, Patricio, having come full circle, is a member of the Pastoral Team in one of our Anglican churches.

Then Omar Ortiz, a national pastor of an Anglican church in Vina del Mar on the coast, gave me an opportunity to blend in some of the Pentecostal power factor to the Anglican framework. He invited me to lead an evangelistic campaign. I had never been given such responsibility or such freedom before, and I set to with some fervour.

Once again, as I prepared, I knew with a glowing certainty that evangelism was what it was all about, as far as I was concerned. I knew God had used me in evangelism, but this wasn't necessarily a big part of my identity until this offer came out of the blue. I worked and prayed through a series of messages based on God's encounters with people, and found this concentrated effort was a welcome relief from the frustrations and tensions which church life in Santiago was causing in me.

That week broke me in as an evangelist. I put my whole heart into it, and the first few days I was plunged into a battle the likes of which I had never known before. Omar and his wife had a lovely home and family, and I enjoyed meeting real Chilean Christians and spending time with them. Yet the picture emerged of a church divided, discouraged, reduced in membership and by no means all supportive of the campaign we were holding. We decided to leave the inviting and publicity to the Lord and just get down to urgent praying. I would pray all morning, and then go over to the church where I encouraged a small band of faithful intercessors.

The visiting evangelist sees aspects of church life not apparent to the leader. Everyone was telling me their problems and difficulties, all the personality conflicts came out, and here I was looking for some solid backing! The first few days hardly anyone came to the meetings, and when I stepped out in great faith and asked for people to come forward for prayer, no-one came. Night after night this went on.

Wednesday was the low point. I was obviously not only wasting my time, but making a very public fool of myself and God. On Thursday morning I jumped off a bus which was still moving quite fast, thinking that if it killed me I didn't care because God couldn't use me. No-one had prepared me for the discouragement and depression which I now recognise as part of the job.

The hall felt like quite a different place when I got there on Thursday. Several different churches sent groups so that the place was full. The theme of my preaching that night was Christ's victory over the Devil, based on the story of the Gadarene swine. As I preached, I saw God's hand moving over the people, and then the glory came down and God started to move in wonderful power. There were people converted, others healed, others filled with the Spirit. I was swept up in events much larger than myself: God was at work! I just moved around doing what seemed best, but aware that if I had gone home they would all have carried on. Not that wild horses could have driven me away. I had been waiting for this all week.

As I prepared on Friday I felt a holy fire burning within me. I found myself praying for the people who had shared their problems with me, and that night was an occasion of great repentance and sanctification of the church. The purifying holy power of God burned in people so strongly that they confessed their sins, received his forgiveness, and many problems in the church seemed to be ironed out. Many backsliders felt God's love again, and deep hurts were healed.

I just knew that Sunday was going to be special, the last golden brush stroke that would complete the picture. As I stood in front of a packed church quite lost in worship and caught up with the Lord, I knew the fulfilment of the evangelist. The hard work of a campaign like that is done before the first hymn is sung. The battle begins before in prayer. It was a wonderful time for me, and I sensed it was to be the first of many.

Being an evangelist probably never was easy, but as a profession we have certainly taken some big knocks in recent years. Excesses and distortions and corruptions among evangelists have been widely publicised, and since most of the public don't understand our motives in the first place, evangelism as a concept sways between a huge ego trip and a high-handed holier-than-thou stuffing of unpalatable thoughts down people's throats and making them feel guilty.

Some months after this campaign I had to learn another hard lesson: the disillusionment of the re-visiting evangelist. So few of those who had apparently been converted were still in contact with the church. The tensions and personality conflicts had returned, in some cases multiplied, and all that glory and power had seemingly faded to nothing. That really set me thinking.

I compared notes with other campaigns, and saw how common a situation this was. Something was obviously wrong. We thought we were building for eternity, and the results were lasting a few weeks. We were trying to give God the glory, but the overall atmosphere in the long run was one of gloom and hopelessness.

In my times of prayer up on the hill overlooking Santiago I began to envision these small, self-multiplying churches. How were they to grow? Was it the follow-up that was lacking? Well, yes, in a way, it had to be, but how could it be improved? Gradually, I was feeling my way towards the idea that outreach should not be some amazing five-yearly event in the life of the church, a great spasm which took everyone by surprise and from which they recovered as soon as possible and returned to their usual ways of doing things. Evangelism should be a way of life, part of the normal church structures and methods. A campaign of the other sort could be mounted once in a while, to give your programmes a boost, but then the impulse is not lost. You disciple the fruit, store it away in the barns and prepare the soil for the next harvest.

Although my thinking was becoming a little clearer, little of this percolated through to what I actually did every day. I carried on the work in La Florida, my involvement with the Holanda group remained confused, and I also helped Gordon and Beryl where I could. They organised a holiday club for children which was remarkably fruitful: the parents came along to watch what the children had been doing, and this provided a talking point so that some families were drawn into Bible study groups.

Many of the Whitehead's neighbours, nominally Catholic but with no live connection with their church, were fascinated by a few films and discussions. The months of integrating themselves into the neighbourhood had really paid off for Gordon and Beryl. There were several solid conversions, and the first church was born in the Barrio Alto. We called it the Monte Olympo church, and it had about ten to twenty in the congregation on an average Sunday. I was not often there, because my priority was with La Florida, but occasionally I was invited to preach, and it had all the signs of a well-established group. One down–nine to go!

Something similar had begun too in the Bazeley household. Though encouraging, these house-churches were also very weak. If a fire-engine passed by the whole ceremony would stop as everyone rushed to the door to see where the fire was!

As we reflected on these goings-on as a team, we developed the concept of evangelism to include the day-to-day living out of the gospel among the neighbours. I thought of it as lifestyle evangelism, and this meshed nicely with the need for the church to be structured for constant growth. Ordinary people were to be involved in outreach, in fact they were the best people to do it, and it could be a completely natural part of their lives.

Later this developed into a carefully programmed strategy summed up in the adage, 'New believers bring new believers'. Many Latin American churches have a series of evangelistic outreaches: three, four, even ten in a year, following each one with intensive discipling of the new believers. They are taught to live out their faith naturally, and, of course, to bring their family and friends to the next outreach. And so it mushrooms on...

I had now been in Chile for a year, and I was still living with the Whiteheads. I had made plenty of mistakes and learned many lessons. Now God was ready to show me a whole new section of the jigsaw puzzle of my life–definitely the sweetest thing so far!

# CHAPTER EIGHT

# FROM MONO TO STEREO

In an idle moment, I was flicking through Gordon and Beryl's record collection when I came across a cover which had me transfixed. It was of a group who called themselves Los Picaflores (The Hummingbirds). All four musicians came from the same family, called Barratt, who were missionaries with SAMS as I was. I had seen this record back in England, before I dreamed of ever returning to Chile, and it had a mesmeric effect on me even then. Was it just because I had seen it before that I was so transfixed? One face in particular stood out: a sweet and delightful face framed in long dark hair and smiling out at the camera from behind a Paraguayan harp.

'Who is this?' I asked Beryl, trying to sound nonchalant.

'Oh, that's Hilary Barratt,' she replied, 'the only one of the family that hasn't married yet.' I knew immediately that this was good news for me. I had never felt such a powerful attraction for any person, let alone a photo. I struggled to keep my voice level.

'Where do they live?'

'Oh, in Argentina, as far as I know.' Was Beryl's nonchalance as studied as mine?

'Just wondered...' I glanced once more at that lovely face, smiling as if for me alone, and tucked the record back in the rack, already planning to go to Argentina as soon as funds and work-load permitted.

One of the first areas of my life to come under scrutiny after my conversion had been my attitude to women. I just didn't know how to relate to them as people. Before I became a Christian, it didn't occur to me that my aims in a relationship were essentially selfish and irresponsible. Once I looked over the past with God's eyes, I decided the best thing to do was to steer clear of women completely. After a while, I discovered the joys of having women as friends, with no worldly act to put on, and no sub-agendas. What a release! Yet I knew I was no celibate, and several homes, including Beryl and Gordon's, had filled me with longing to have a wife and family of my own.

Because of the great influence they had on my life, I thought my cousin Rosemary and her husband David had something to teach me here. They had told me that they waited seven years to get married, which seemed biblical enough. Seven years, starting from my conversion, would bring me to 1976. It was now the last days of 1975. For seven years I had prayed intermittently about God's plan for my wife, and to show I meant business I hadn't got involved in a steady relationship, and knew I wouldn't do so until God showed me that this was the one. Is that what he was saying now? And how soon could I get to Argentina?

The very next day, Arthur Robinson asked me to go out with him to La Florida, across town, for a funeral.

It was a solemn occasion. One of our congregation who had been converted in the south of Chile and then moved to Santiago, had taken a job in Tucuman, Argentina. His wife, still living in Santiago, had been told that tragically he had been killed in an accident involving electricity. She had made her way across the Andes to bring back his body in an ambulance, and the church there, forewarned, had sent somebody to travel back with her.

We walked from the blinding summer sunlight of Chile's December into the wooden shack of a church, where the weight of the widow's grief was almost palpable around us. And there stood Hilary, the girl from the record.

She was every bit as lovely as the photo, and it was almost overwhelming to be in the same room, so unexpectedly. I almost couldn't look at her. I decided to look at her hands. 'If they are as beautiful as the rest, then she's the one for me, Lord,' I decided.

I did, they were, and she was.

In a film, the unsanitary surroundings would have gone out of focus, and a string quartet faded in on the soundtrack. This being real life, we had to get through the funeral first. Nevertheless, by the end of the afternoon I had plenty to think about.

This Hilary certainly had some character. The ambulance had broken down over the Andes, and the driver had gone for help. The widow wouldn't leave her husband's body, and Hilary wouldn't leave her, so she had spent most of Christmas day locked in an abandoned ambulance on a remote mountain pass with a corpse and a grieving widow.

On the other hand, I also gathered that her relationship with God had taken a back seat over the last few years, and that there was some relationship in Argentina she was running away from. Having imagined I would marry an on-fire-for-the-Lord Pentecostal type, this rocked me severely. I played it very cool in her presence, and over the following days, as her name ran round and round in my brain, I tried to turn my thoughts into prayers that God would guide us. On the human level, she was perfect for me: was this the ultimate temptation?

Certainly, she seemed to be in no hurry to return to Argentina. We kept meeting all over the place. She recommitted her life to Christ. This was wonderful, yet I was still not satisfied. It took a whole readjustment of my spiritual values, and a certain humility to accept that perhaps I was more demanding than God was. I had spiritual hurdles for her to overcome that were just inappropriate for her, and I had also blinded myself to the idea that I could learn anything from her spiritually.

When she joined the Holanda group, I was delighted to see her joining in the worship, and weeping a lot as she sang. I concluded that God was dealing deeply with her, and rejoiced. She just radiated love and acceptance to everyone in a way that became increasingly unbearable for me. We got on so well. Now there were two burning issues in my mind: what was I to do about the Anglican church, and what about Hilary? I confided in David Prior, who was visiting at the time, and promised to pray.

The summer holidays, which run over the Christmas period in the Southern hemisphere, were coming to an end. She had to go back, because she had nowhere to live and no job. Yet still she did not go. The day before she was due to return, it was agreed that she could stay with Ray and Gill Smith, but there was still a job to be found. She was trained as a P E teacher.

Wanting to hang on to her, I tried the obvious but unpromising step of contacting local schools a week before term began.

'Do you have a teaching post, by any chance?' I asked the first Head Teacher on my list, in Spanish, having decided this was more appropriate.

'No, I'm afraid we've nothing suitable for you,' was the reply. 'We only have one vacancy and that is for a female P E teacher who speaks English.' Suddenly, neither language would obey me. Then I pulled my stunned senses together.

'I might just be able to help you.'

Hilary didn't so much apply for that job as claim it.

It took little time before we were engaged, although privately at first. We still had a few ups and downs to get over, and this unresolved relationship in Argentina to sort out. Yet behind it all, everything was so passionately right. And we made a great team.

We began to play harp and guitar together. The harp was such a mesmeric, joyful ripple of music that people sat, transfixed by it. It expressed all the closeness to nature, the daily struggles and the unquenchable love of life of the Andean people. It drew people out of themselves, reminded them of the power and symetry of creation, the beauty and the mystery of life. By the time Hilary had finished playing, her audience was like putty in my hands. It was the best warm-up technique I could have wished for as an evangelist. Without a word, the music raised the questions for which Jesus was the only answer.

Omar Ortiz, who had invited me to lead the evangelistic campaign earlier, asked me to return to his other church, and Hilary came with me. The two burning questions I had asked David Prior to pray about were, what about Hilary, and what about the Anglican church? It was really during this campaign that I realised that in giving me the answer to the first question, God had also provided the key to the second.

Hilary was Anglican, and in her I saw all the love and maturity of the team I was working with. I saw the extraordinary humility it takes to divest yourself of your own culture and spiritual identity and to immerse yourself lovingly in another culture. Having grown up in Chile, Paraguay and Argentina, Hilary brought together the dynamic Pentecostal insights with the simple charismatic Anglicanism in a blend that seemed perfect to me. The prayer and praise of the Pentecostals on Montserrat, which had become an indelible root of my own spirituality, was also the source of the doctrinal instability and emotional excesses which had worried me in the Holanda group when they got involved with Renovacion. Now in Hilary, and in Omar, I found the path which lay between the two, and which felt right to me. Perhaps I had a future with these dear Anglicans after all.

All this was more than a rational process. It was a love affair. As the evening meeting got under way in Omar's church I would look across the platform at this angel with her harp, and while she radiated God's love to the people there she would smile her special love for me. Then I would grab my Bible and preach my heart out, loving God's word and thrilled to see people respond. I knew she was praying for them and for me as I preached, and we both felt carried on a wave of God's love as we ministered together. Then afterwards, despite the exhaustion, we would talk and kiss and tell each other how grateful to God we were for each other. It felt like heaven. I had never been so fulfilled, as a person or as a Christian.

'Gordon, I've come to a decision.'

Gordon looked up from his cup of coffee, surprised perhaps by the momentous tone of my voice. It was the end of a hard day for him, but he was ready, as always, to listen. A raised eyebrow was all the invitation I needed.

'I'd like to sign up for your confirmation class.'

He laughed, not at me, but at the rightness of it. Yet he couldn't resist teasing me a little.

'Is that all? I thought you were going to ask me to marry you tomorrow because you'd got fed up with waiting. OK, I'll put you on the list. Are you sure? You've only been with us a couple of years. I don't want to rush you.'

I was still serious. 'God spoke to me tonight.'

'It was a good evening, wasn't it?' Together we were leading the first ever retreat for the first church in the Barrio Alto. About thirty members of the church had gone away together to explore what God had in mind for them, individually and as a group. The warmth and sense of purpose, as well as fulfilment, was enormous.

'I looked around at all these people as they prayed, and God said, "This is your family." This is where he wants me. It's not enough to be committed just to the worldwide church. So I've made a love-commitment to join you officially.'

'Don't tell me the freewheeling individualist Alf Cooper is going to conform at last!'

'Oh no, I'll never conform. Just because I'm in your net it doesn't mean I'm going to stop wriggling!'

Gordon groaned. 'That was too much to ask. Never

mind, we've coped with you so far.' Then a thought suddenly struck him. 'Would Hilary have anything to do with this, by any chance?'

I beamed: even hearing her name made me smile.

'She's got everything to do with it, and nothing.'

It all seemed to happen so fast, but there was no point in delaying once we were sure. Over Easter we went on a wonderful trip to a Scripture Union camp in Peru, then on to Tucuman in Argentina to meet her parents. How great was our joy when Tony Barratt, Hilary's dad and my hero, the most tender and brilliant Christian I have ever known, married us back in Chile. It was April the 9th: we had met less than four months before.

We had a wonderful honeymoon on the Chilean coast, all glorious sunsets, screeching sea-gulls, lazy sunny beaches and roaring oceans. Once back in Santiago we found a beautiful little house which became our nest, and it was just sheer bliss. Or at least, sheer bliss with a little adjusting to do. The speed with which our lives had come together meant that while we had little physical baggage, there was a lot of emotional baggage to unpack.

I didn't find it easy to communicate my feelings, especially the negative ones. My life so far had trained me to be fairly self-contained. I adjusted easily to telling Hilary how much I loved her, but had little experience of expressing resentments or fears when they arose. Perhaps I thought they shouldn't be there, so I should ignore them and hope they would go away. This was a lousy solution.

Hilary didn't believe that a home was a home without a cat, and once there, a cat was to be fondled tenderly. She did this instinctively, without realising that within a week I was in a torment of jealousy over that cat. It seemed so stupid that I couldn't say anything about it. Then one night as I watched her with this confounded animal I thought I was going to choke with rage. Having been bottled up for so long, there was quite an explosion, and the whole horrible mess came out. Hilary, quite unprepared for this outburst, did the best possible thing: she burst into laughter, and the next minute we were laughing in each other's arms. That was my first lesson: communicate the negatives.

The second lesson was not so easy and took longer: we needed to forgive each other for our past. I found that the thought of the relationship she had broken off in Argentina disturbed me, and Hilary suffered over my past relationships, long over though they were. I would give anything to re-live my life in the knowledge that the best is worth waiting for. I impress this on all the youth groups I talk to, and suggest that a handful of good friendships should be the norm until God definitely brings the right person into your life. Yet this is so personal, and so difficult to discern.

In my lectures I gave on marriage before I met Hilary, I had thought that the injunction 'Do not let the sun go down on your wrath' should be obeyed. I was a great one for rules. Now I discovered that this was more than a good idea, it was a necessity for us. We simply could not end the day if anything was amiss between us.

Yet spiritually we were so different. I would get up at six o'clock, shower, pray for an hour, and then take a sleepy Hilary tea in bed. Where was the discipline in this?

'What's so wonderful about discipline?' she would ask. 'I prayed last night, so I'm several hours ahead of you.'

Of course we had discussed these differences, but somehow actually living with the reality still left a lot of thinking to do. Talking about it would be like picking our way through a minefield, but sooner or later we had to try. I handed over the mug of tea and sat down on the bed.

'The thing is,' I began with a deep breath, 'my whole Christian life is based on a minimum of an hour's prayer in the morning. Tony Grant drummed that into me back at the beginning when I first knew the Lord. Are you saying that all those cold early mornings, those days when it seemed so difficult to start praying—are you saying that they are optional? Have I swallowed what he said without thinking and gone on doing it like a robot over the years?'

'Oh Alf,' Hilary smiled wryly as she took my hand. 'I do love you. I can see you're bending over backwards not to be judgemental. You know the answer to that: sometimes it's hard, but it brings you such joy, and that's the way you know the Lord. If you didn't pray in the mornings it would be like trying to build a marriage without talking to me. I understand why you do it. I admire you for it. I love you because of it. I'm not asking you to change. The question is, are you hoping that I'm going to change?'

'No!' I answered quickly. 'Well, perhaps...but no. I don't think so. It's just that you're my wife. Bone of my bone and all that...'

'What if I weren't your wife? What do you think of all those Christians out there who launch off into the day with a vague Godward thought as they feed the cat?' She looked at me mischievously. 'If people who feed cats can be Christians at all, that is.'

'You leave your cat out of this,' I snapped, playing

her game. I thought for a moment. 'I've never wanted to make people feel that I was judging them, but some obviously did feel threatened. At All Nations I was quite astonished to find that all those missionary trainees really didn't pray very much at all, by my standards. They didn't seem worried by it. I thought I would encourage them, but they couldn't cope with me talking about it. I suppose I thought it made them feel guilty.'

'I expect it did, Alf. Everyone knows that people who love God pray to him: so those who pray most must love him most. And maybe he loves them most. And maybe they'll get into heaven first. That's it! I only married you because I think I can slip into heaven on your ticket.'

'You are such a tease,' I grinned. 'I'm trying to have a serious conversation here, and you keep making me want to kiss you.'

'Nothing more serious than that,' countered Hilary, kissing me seriously. She really wasn't helping my train of thought.

Reluctantly I escaped. 'I'm not saying that our salvation depends on praying in the morning. And from God's point of view there aren't "real" Christians and "unspiritual" Christians: either you are saved by his grace or not at all. But they're missing out on so much. Above all, how can they work for him without knowing his power which comes through deep times of prayer? You know, I've been on missions with people, and I've seen them come straight down to breakfast and get on with the day, and I thought they would pray afterwards. No, they don't. After dinner they disappear and I think, "Aha, that's when they pray"—then I find them snoozing in the sun. We get to the evening, when they are leading a great evangelistic rally, and they have only spent a while in prayer with the team. No time alone with God that I can see at all. It's like setting out on a long journey over the desert with an empty fuel tank...is that judgemental?'

'Well, it was beginning to sound a bit like a sermon,' admitted Hilary. 'But it needs saying. The thing is, if you are feeling judgemental, that's how people are going to take it. I would say that I pray all day, and that an hour in the morning would kill all my joy. Surely what matters is that I know I am in constant touch with God. It works for me, and for lots of other people. I call it quite a different system; you call it no system at all. It'll take a while for both of us to come to terms with that. God must have married us off so that you are forced to accept another kind of spirituality, to teach you a bit of humility.'

'Oh, you're knocking the corners off me, all right,' I sighed. 'But can you cope with the pressure of my expectations now that we've discussed it a bit?'

'I'm quite secure, thank you. I can cope with your expectations, and I even appreciate your encouragement in my spiritual life–sometimes. The rest of the time I'll do it my way. If the pressure gets to me, I'll tell you. Meanwhile, perhaps you could remove the pressure of you sitting on my bed so I can get up.

'OK,' I nodded gravely. 'I'll leave you alone so you can pray.'

Certainly in terms of a natural walk with Christ, Hilary seems to have had this bred into her. She walks Christ. She radiates love and acceptance at people, and draws them to God. She reaches people who wouldn't listen to me for two minutes. One day she told me that a teacher at the school had confided that she didn't think she could go on living with the loneliness and guilt of marital infidelity.

'What an opportunity!' I enthused. 'Did you offer to pray with her?'

'No, Alf, I just listened. There was so much pain there, so many shattered hopes. She wasn't ready to pray: she just needed to cry.'

'Have you invited her round for a meal?' I knew this was a key card in Hilary's hand. She loved entertaining, and we often prayed that our home would be a place where people would find God.

'Not yet. She needs more time to talk by herself, to one person, to sort her ideas out. At the moment she's coping by not thinking about it, but she feels as though she's living on a volcano. This morning was just the beginning. In fact, she couldn't really relax in the staff-room where anyone could walk in at any moment. And she doesn't know me very well, either. Why should she talk to me? I just asked if she had any friends or family who would listen, and told her I would be very happy to meet her outside school if that's what she wanted. I couldn't rush her.'

'You mean, you just left the situation like that, with nothing decided, and her running off to some pagan cousin?'

'Oh, Alf, where is your faith? We'll pray. Either she'll come running back to me, when she chooses, or her cousin will turn out to be a raving Pentecostal, or the situation will get so bad that she'll find herself praying of her own accord.'

There it was again. The Anglican 'softly softly' approach, which I had sometimes thought so feeble, but backed up with the faith which made it work...eventually.

'I'm sorry, I'm just an evangelist. I'd have grabbed the situation by the throat and she wouldn't have spoken to me again. You're quite right. What's better, put off ninety per cent by slamming in there with the full gospel in the first conversation, or lose fifty per cent because the situation drifts?'

'There's a place for what you do Alf.'

'But I think back to Montserrat, where I gave myself so much pain because I was so inflexible, so much in a hurry to reap the harvest. I put everyone's back up. You would just have loved them all, and they would have loved you.'

'But I would never have launched out into the preaching tours, and seen so many people come to Christ. That was the Pentecostal way. My way is more Anglican. What we both need is discernment to know what is needed in each case. I tend one way, you tend the other. Together, we make one decent Christian—a Pentecostal Anglican.'

True spirituality is love: this is what Hilary taught me. Hours and hours of prayer were vital. Without prayer little seemed to happen: but without love nothing was authentically Christian. So many of my failures in evangelism had come from trying to steamroller people into the Kingdom. Because I was so 'on fire for the Lord' there was a distance between me and non-Christians. Hilary was completely at ease with them. I loved them because in some sense they were the 'enemy', and Christ told me to love them. Hilary loved them as they were without having a spiritual reason for it.

Over the first few months we contacted several people in the neighbourhood, and eventually held what we called a 'Bible Encounter Group' in our home. It was exactly what I would have wanted, but I needed to learn another way, which I now see as Christ's way. I had to learn how to love creatively, continually. Sometimes I couldn't see what to do next: the answer was to love.

The early days of our marriage were such a rich time, with all the pieces of the jigsaw coming together. The outward circumstances of my life all dovetailed together, and all my spiritual experiences, which had sometimes seemed to be scattered and pulling in different directions, now built up into one great and glorious whole. Emotionally, life had changed from black and white into colour. All this, just for me!

Yet I knew also that however much God swamped me with his love, it would never feel right to me not to share it with others. The new sensitivity to others that I was learning through Hilary had echoes in my thoughts on evangelism: a loving home was the natural stepping stone between an encounter on the street and a visit to my church. On a more theoretical level, the meshing of the Anglican and Pentecostal styles had an immediate impact on my work, bringing a new conviction and rightness to my position in the team.

It was no great surprise to me when Colin suggested one day that I should be ordained, although there were questions.

'Can you just be ordained, like that? I don't actually know much about Anglicanism.' Colin smiled.

'Technically, you need to be confirmed, which you are, and trained, which you are. As for knowing about Anglicanism, I'll lend you a book. It's not exactly orthodox, but you never were, and South America isn't either. As your bishop, I am quite convinced you should be ordained. We'll give you a sort of curacy here, and a church to work with when you go back to England on home leave. I need more ordained men. Apart from anything else, we're working hard towards national Chilean leadership in the Anglican church–what better half-way house than ordaining an Anglo-Chilean?'

Colin showed his true colours in such moments: kind and humble, he was a true bishop, a master of reconciliation and wise leadership. I had trusted him from the start, and in this matter of ordination, if it was alright with the bishop, it was alright by me.

'Well, I've been confirmed and married by the Anglicans in the last couple of months, so I may as well go for the triple!'

So it was that my dear Granny, who had prayed for me so faithfully, came with great joy to my confirmation, then to my wedding, and very shortly afterwards to my ordination. Shortly after, very peacefully, she died.

God seemed to be starting a new chapter in my life.

CHAPTER NINE

# STOCKTAKE UK

No sooner had I joined them formally, than the Anglican team decided that the timing was about right for Hilary and me to have a period of home leave. The strategy for the next few years was that I was to plant a church in Providencia, which was in the down-town area of the Barrio Alto. Once that had started, it could be difficult to take three to six months out, so it was agreed that we would go to England first.

Home leave, despite what people may think, is far from a holiday: in this case we were to team up with Hilary's brother Terry, and go round as a mini-music group on tour, doing evangelism and encouraging SAMS supporters around the country.

Hilary and Terry, missionary kids all their lives, were quite used to the concept of furlough, of living out of suitcases, being passed around from one church to another, lovingly looked after in each place, but everywhere telling the same stories and starting again with a new set of faces. I felt rootless and awkward, and only

Hilary's love and encouragement soothed me back into the role which was expected of me.

There were many opportunities, of course, to meet up with old friends and compare notes.

'I can't believe how normal you look!' teased Mark as he showed us into his living room. 'There I was, praying for you all this time, and you go and turn into an Anglican Vicar: I tell you, I nearly gave up on you. I suppose it's all your fault,' he smiled at Hilary. 'He must be crazy about you to take such a drastic measure.'

'Oh, he is!' Hilary grinned. 'But actually, the fact that anyone might think that was his motive was quite a problem. I'm sure it was more difficult for him to know that the Anglican church was right for him. He agonised about it enough, as you know from his prayer letters. But he got his priorities straight in the end.' She tried to keep a straight face at Mark's expression.

I knew that Mark, like a lot of my friends in England, had found a new freedom in the Spirit by 'opting out' of the established church. If I had stayed in England, I might well have done the same thing. But God led me differently.

'You've been too near the Anglican wood to see the trees,' I argued. 'The Anglican church in Chile is in a wonderful position for growth. It's got all the solid foundations of historic Christianity combined with all the excitement and flexibility of the house churches: best of both worlds, really.'

'You might be right,' admitted Mark grudgingly. 'But what about the liturgy?'

'You said "liturgy" as if it was a crime,' I responded hotly. 'I know you can't imagine me using Anglican liturgy, but it works better than the old hymn sandwich. It's just a lot more flexible.'

In fact, I had felt at home surprisingly soon using a written service: the nominal Roman Catholics were reassured because there was a dignity about it which they expected of church, and we could pour into that framework all the challenge and enthusiasm of the Pentecostals. I had become an Anglican not because I believed it to be the 'only' or even the 'best' church, but because I was sure God had led me there, and I was quite excited about the potential. So, though I felt part of Christ's whole church and very much at home in any Christ-loving congregation, I frequently found myself defending the established church to my house-church friends.

'It's a great boat to fish from,' I concluded.

Talking to Anglicans, quite a different set of questions arose. Most of the SAMS supporters had a grasp of mission to the poor, particularly in rural areas, but had trouble adjusting to the idea of preaching to the middle-class and prosperous areas of Santiago. Eventually I decided to take the bull by the horns, and started talking about 'Evangelism in the Mink and Mercedes set'.

'The *Barrio Alto*, where we are working, is the most status-conscious society you can imagine,' I explained in church services, prayer meetings and missionary coffee mornings up and down the country. 'Some people are born there, mostly wealthy Chilean families descended from the Spaniards. Others have fought for a place and got it through business, or politics, but the main requirement is money—lots of it. You don't talk about money, you just have it.

'You have a big architect-designed house in Santiago, with a swimming pool and an intercom at the gate so no-one can visit without your approval. There is another week-end house in the country or on the coast, and a car for every member of the family who can drive. There are several maids so your wife never cooks, and can spend her time at aerobic classes, and building up a selection of up-to-the-minute clothes and exclusive perfumes. You send your children to Oxbridge if you possibly can, or Harvard and Yale.

'To keep all this show of affluence, you work flat out for twelve hours a day. You fiddle any deal you can, and boast of any form of tax evasion. No deal is too crooked if it works to your advantage: if you get caught, your so-called friends melt away and on your own head be it. You work such long hours that you never see your family, and the strain soon creates its own casualties. Marriages are breaking up all the time, sex and drugs are wreaking havoc among the young, and homosexuality is very fashionable. A good psychiatrist is not just part of the image: anyone who claims to be able to put your life back together has got to be a good thing.'

Yet many of the psychiatrists have nothing to offer. One day I was driving along when a car in front of me very nearly collided with an oncoming van. The young driver spun off the road, out of control, and when I had parked and walked back to see if he was all right, he was just sitting there at the wheel trembling. I offered to drive him home, which he accepted, but compensated for this admittance of weakness by showing off all the way there. He spoke four languages, quoted Shakespeare at me when he heard my English connections, and was dropping names as if his life depended on it. I've never seen such an impressive display of the man who needed nobody. Through his ranting and ravings, I asked God to give me the key.

'Why are you so afraid?' I asked. He burst into tears. Between sobs he admitted that all the showing off was just a way of covering up for his sense that his psychiatry was meaningless. As he directed me through an exclusive neighbourhood, he described some of the detailed study he had done, which had left him with more questions than answers about the human condition.

When we got to his house, he told me he was one of the best-paid psychiatrists in the country.

'I know the best in the world,' I said, playing his name-dropping game. 'He is Doctor Jesus.'

As we talked, the Holy Spirit poured his life into the conversation and before I left this man had given his heart to the Lord. If the mess of his life was any indication of what psychiatrists can do, then God help those who go there for the answer.

Having painted for my British audience this picture of the affluent but needy, I could then ask the question I had heard so many times before, because now the answer was obvious.

'Is it ridiculous to think of bringing the love of Jesus to these people? Does a missionary have to restrict his activities only to the poor, the unemployed and the uneducated? How about reaching those who shape society in Latin America?'

Then I would go on to share our experiences of how the gospel was now making in-roads to that sector of society where it had scarcely been heard before, and how with the new churches we had learned new lessons on how to do evangelism.

In Chile I had asked the first Barrio Alto converts

what they thought the best way would be to evangelise this sector of the city. I had expected the usual methods—visiting door-to-door, preaching in the open air, and so on. But they had other ideas.

'It's obvious,' they said. 'Barbecues.'

And they were quite right. Delicious barbecues, with a natural mix of Christians and their non-Christian friends have become the main-stay of our evangelism, and always turn into beautiful sharing times. Many have come to Christ by hearing reasoned testimonies at these naturally joyful social occasions. It works because cultural 'insiders' set the agenda. In other parts of Chile, among the Mapuche Indians where other SAMS missionaries are working, they use other methods. Evangelism and evangelistic methods need to be constantly refined, tuned to find the best means by which as many as possible can comfortably hear about Jesus, and see lives changed by Jesus in their own culture.

Methods must also meet the needs. We detected the number one social need in the Barrio Alto: strengthening the family and particularly marriages. A Catholic version of a system called Marriage Encounter adapted well, and today at any one time we have waiting lists which could fill the next two or three Marriage Encounter Week-ends. These are people who have no contact with the church, who have been intrigued by the story of friends who have been through the teaching. Many find Christ as well as a new start in their marriages, and when they do, a whole family walks into church next Sunday.

These experiences taught us that concern for the people and zeal for the Lord were only the starting points for evangelism: these needed to be modified so that evangelism was culturally sensitive, so people felt comfortable. As we visited churches in the UK we were able to encourage them with our stories, but not so that they tried to follow the Chilean pattern. They needed to work out patterns of evangelism which were culturally appropriate for them.

At St Andrew's, Chorleywood, where we were sent for a parish placement, we worked out with a lay evangelist friend a method of parish visitation and outreach. This allowed the church to sow seed in the parish regularly, and to find those spiritually hungry people that the Mormons and Jehovah's Witnesses so often pick up.

Many churches were rather discouraged about evangelism, but only needed a little encouragement in the directions they were already taking. We were overjoyed to see the results of evangelism in Britain as well.

From their conversion, the Christians in Chile are expected to do evangelism. They might make all sorts of theological blunders, but the passion is there, and their new-found love for God is contagious. Their 'good news' is hot off the press. All their friends and family are wondering what is happening, and they are taught to explain simply what it means to come to Christ, and to invite anybody interested first to something like a barbecue where they can meet Christians, then later to a church service.

There is a 'bare wires' approach to evangelism in Chile. The insulation with which we so often protect ourselves from the power of the gospel—feeling shy or inadequate to explain our faith, fear of seeming holier than thou, not wanting to impose on people—all this seems to be stripped away in their enthusiasm to share Jesus.

While there is the same need to be culturally sensitive to British culture, we found that Christians in the UK who were motivated to take the brakes off their faith and to find their own way forward in evangelism were encouraged by the results. And so were we!

CHAPTER TEN

# CHURCHES, CHURCHES, CHURCHES

We returned to Chile encouraged and refreshed, and ready to start serious church planting. There was plenty of theory in my head, and I had expounded it all to anyone who would listen while we were on furlough: now we had to do it.

At least we had a building–the English community church where all the Anglo-Chileans had been baptised and married for years. Usually I would have considered the building less important than the people, but in this case the existence of the building also laid the foundations of the congregation. We worked through the registers at the church and contacted everyone we could, letting them know that we were going to start a service in Spanish. Most of them were obviously no more interested in Christ than many people who opt for church weddings, but it was a start. In addition, we were being loaned a few young Christians from both Gordon and Beryl's group, and from Colin and Barbara's.

Humanly speaking, we weren't starting from a position of power. I thought back to La Florida, and remembered the first few meetings in Enrique and Merla's cramped kitchen, with a schizophrenic and a mentally handicapped child. That church was still growing strongly: by comparison this foundation was palatial.

Yet without prayer, watering the tiny seeds of life in the people we had contacted, there was no hope. We prayed over the registers of names, we prayed as we phoned and visited. Still there was something missing. I needed God's strong confirmation on all this. I decided to give God a prayer to answer.

'Lord, I still have my doubts about tackling this job in such an Anglican way, so logically. If this is your way for us, and we've understood your will, I want one person to come to the first service who has nothing to do with our efforts. I want you to bring them in by your sovereign power, and bring them to faith in you. This is the fleece I'm laying down, your seal on this work, so that I can be sure that I'm one hundred percent in the centre of your will.'

The Sunday of the first service dawned, and Hilary and I started with prayer in the building. We didn't expect to fill more than the first couple of rows, so I wouldn't use the platform: I put a little straw-seated chair facing them. The numbers weren't important, but I was clinging to the conversation I had claimed, drawing some unknown person to the church.

Maria Eliana came from one of the luxurious houses nearby, but she had little emotional security. She was the daughter of one of the maids in the house: she and her mother had been abandoned by her alcoholic father, and their employer had taken pity on them. She had been brought up in the family, and sent to school by them. She turned out to be very bright, and had worked her way through University, succeeding beyond her dreams as a commercial banker. Money was no problem now, but in the centre of her life was an aching void, the memory of her alcoholic father. She had tried several churches, first Catholic, and then Methodist, but nothing seemed to meet even her need for friends, let alone the spiritual hunger. That morning, she too had laid down a fleece for the God she hardly dared believe in.

'God, I'm going to one more church today. This is your last chance. If I don't find you there, I'm not going to look any more.'

So the two prayers locked together, mine and Maria Eliana's, and as she walked around not really knowing where to go next, she heard the sound of our opening hymn, and pushed the door slightly ajar. Hilary, who had posted herself at the back with the hymn books, was still hovering at the door for late-comers, and drew her in with smiles. Then, sensing that there would be no more arrivals, she followed her to her seat and sat beside her. As the service got into full swing, the tears started to fall down Maria Eliana's cheeks, and by the end she was ready to give her heart to God. As together Hilary and I prayed with her, and heard her thank Jesus for the love which she had failed to find in her earthly father, I also had a prayer of thanksgiving.

'Thank you, Lord. Now I know I'm on the right track.'

This was only the beginning, the first convert at the first service of the first church I myself planted. Three years later, that congregation was one hundred strong when we left it for our next home leave, and each member came because Christ met them at their point of need, just like Maria Eliana.

In the years since Maria Eliana wept her way through the first Spanish service at Providencia I have seen many, many people led to Christ. It is always fresh, always a miracle, and my deepest motivation.

But suddenly, when I had a church for new converts to relate to, many threads of my thinking began to come together. I had always realised of course that evangelism is not an end in itself. You cannot bring someone to new birth and expect them to survive by themselves any more than you would leave a new-born baby in a dustbin. But now the fuller needs of the new converts became urgent to us. Maria Eliana, with her history of economic and emotional poverty, needed to be grafted into a set of relationships to find wholeness and integration of her life as a Christian. She needed a secure basis for her spiritual life if it were to have any sticking power.

Although it was a great thrill on evangelistic campaigns to see people coming to Christ, mending relationships and seeing the power and the glory of God at work, it was all undermined in my eyes when six months later I discovered that whatever fruit came of such a mission had withered. This was no way to spread the Kingdom of God. Evangelism should not be a hiccough in the life of the church, but the natural expression of the love and the power that the congregation are experiencing all the time.

In my courses at All Nations I had studied principles of church planting: now I could really see the need for not just picking individuals off the streets, but establishing congregations. Gradually the evangelist in me had come to see a wider strategy: evangelism had brought me to the door of church planting. You can convert people one at a time, but the Kingdom of God is built by church-planting.

Lessons I had spent a long time learning now came into focus in a new way. Hilary had taught me that lifestyle evangelism works better than Bible-bashing: this lifestyle was most easily shown in a network of relationships within a church. All my concern over charismatic groups who had lost their sense of balance had taught me that the anointing of the Spirit works hand in glove with strategic planning: a church was needed to live this out. From now on, the name of the game was church-planting.

But just what sort of churches, I wondered, need planting? As we prayed, Hilary and I with the team, we knew that they needed to be self-sustaining, self-multiplying congregations. New converts needed to see themselves as workers and leaders, engaged in evangelism from the start. This is only possible when Jesus is taught to them in a way that changes their own lives first.

Once committed to the church, the new convert goes through a fairly extensive time of ministry which we call a Beginners' Group. Pastoral and spiritual problems are ironed out, and there is often need for a ministry of deliverance through prayer. Every new Christian has sins, weaknesses and habits that need to be moulded into a whole new lifestyle, and only being part of a living expression of the body of Christ can do that at a depth which makes it stick. The first year is spent in basic Christian teaching: how to live, how to love their spouses, how to bring up their kids, how to avoid temptation at the office, and how to balance their monthly budgets. As they learn these, worship, fellowship and evangelism simply overflow.

At the same time they are expected to reach their family and friends for Christ. They might make all sorts of theological blunders, but the passion is there, and their new-found love for God is contagious in a way which can so easily lose its shine if you bury them in Bible Study before you let them loose. Their 'good news' is hot off the press. New believers, encouraged and guided in the right way, are the best at making more new believers.

When a person comes to Christ, apart from the tremendous change in their own lives, there is a whole 'golden seam of evangelism' open to them–their friends, acquaintances, work-mates and family. In Chile, where the extended family is much more import-ant, cousins and grannies, parents and nephews are all intrigued by what is going on, and all suddenly become reachable through him. You can mine this 'golden seam of evangelism' for all it is worth. The new converts want their families to find the same joy as they have, and they provide prayer power and personal contact: the church just organises a social occasion where those friends and relations can meet Christians.

David Mario, for instance. As his generous heart was captured for Jesus and the Holy Spirit jolted him he became a natural. He learned to love his wife, pay taxes and share Jesus. He'd phone me around Wednesday, in great excitement.

'Pastor, pray. I've got one in the frying pan.' I knew this meant he'd made a good contact. Around Friday I'd receive a second phone call.

'Pastor, you can start praising–he's fried!' That meant that on Sunday I could expect David Mario to bring a new believer to church. When you get many such spontaneous witnesses, your church grows spontaneously!

It took several more years to develop a complete programme of training which mobilised the whole church, but from now on I knew this was where I was heading. No one man can do all the evangelism, all the discipling, and all the counselling, and God never intended that it should be like that.

One concept which had intrigued me at All Nations was that of 'extension study' programmes, training people as workers and leaders where they were, rather than taking them off to Bible college. Now that thread of thinking had literally come home to me. Hilary's father, Tony Barratt, while in South America, had pioneered and built up a most amazing study programme known as 'SEAN'—Study by Extension for All Nations. In so many situations across South America where church leadership and theological training were the big bottle-necks as far as church growth was concerned, SEAN had provided the solution. The Bible-college brought to the local church. A combination of serious structured Bible study pitched at the appropriate level, combined with practical work on the streets in evangelism, counselling, social work programmes—that was the way forward. For many years, church leaders had been trained this way: now we started to train *everyone*.

Once they have been through a Beginners' Group, our church members continue in their Bible study, but also start on practical courses to give a sense of purpose and achievement. Confirmation is taken very seriously in our church: I tell them when I prepare them that this is the most important ordination they will ever receive, even if they go on to become a bishop: the ordination of the laity.

At the beginning of each year our members find their names on a call-up list, indicating to which SEAN study they have been assigned. This programme of Growth and Ministry for the laity progresses gradually through a carefully planned curriculum aimed at training every church member in the basics of Bible and ministry. The results are dynamic and fruitful. Couples like Willy and Virginia, and Fernando and Ximene are back-bone material. Among the first to graduate from the Beginners Group, they learned their basics year by year in the SEAN programme and by later teaching such groups. As they ministered they became experts. They are only eight-year-old Christians but have been capable of moving massive numbers to Christ, pillars of Marriage Encounter groups, first-rate Christian workers. They're not perfect, but I'd have to go a long way to find such good workers: they really know what they are doing, because they learned the job on the job.

Churches need to develop a 'life-style of evangelism'. You can't expect family members or friends to be too willing to come to church immediately, but a barbecue is a different matter. They wouldn't listen to a sermon from a recognised 'pastor', but when all their relatives and new friends in the church have, and learn to share, a lively testimony, newcomers usually get the message in a palatable form. We have found the evangelism that works is the continuous, every member, sparkle and testimony dinner-party kind. It keeps on bringing people in all the year round, whether we are holding special evangelistic services or not. This evangelism only works when believers are excited about what is happening to them and in their church. This excitement develops when God is manifestly present in services, changed lives, big and small miracles. And the key to God's manifest presence, in my experience, is much prayer.

Over the years, when outlining the basics of the work in Chile, I have come down to five points.

Firstly, the passion to tell others about Christ, which grew in me from the day of my conversion, needs to be tuned into the culture and the needs of the people you want to reach.

Secondly, new converts need to be discipled in a way which changes their lives for Christ, for ever.

At the same time as the discipling comes the mobilising: lay evangelists from the start, church members can be trained on the job into positions of leadership, gaining experience in every area of the church's ministry simply by doing it, first with our guidance, then under the direct guidance of the Spirit.

This is backed up by extended teaching through the SEAN programme, so that new leaders are trained to be faithful and fruitful.

Finally, this process comes round full circle as we are now beginning to send workers abroad to Spain to plant new churches.

These are very much the bare bones of our work in Chile, and there is so much more that could be written. The growth continues, and the story of this growth has taught us much, much more. Another book will have to tell the story.

This book has described how God dealt with one of his very imperfect but willing workers. I now thank God for the way he guided me through all the hurdles. He met me in my search for a meaning to life on the Spanish road as a callow teenager. He eased my strong-willed individualistic personality into expressions of faith appropriate to me. He allowed me to make all the mistakes in the book while I was still hidden away on Montserrat. He sent me to All Nations Christian College, which provided me with just the tools for the job before I could know quite what the job was going to be. He lead me to the Anglican church, and presented it in the form of Hilary! From there on, hand in hand, we have walked together where we saw God leading and learned to trust him to use us for his glory.

Even though much of my learning was a painful process, God has knocked corners off me, knocked self-reliance out of me, and taught me at every step that he knows best what he is doing and where I am going. Those early years, full of blunders though they may have been, were good years. Through them God has built foundations which have proved true and reliable.

And the Kingdom grows on...Praise God!

# THE SINNER'S PRAYER

'God, I need you and want to meet with you personally.
I know I have offended you and others by my selfish
thoughts, words, deeds, my sin. Thank you that you
love me despite these things. Thank you that you paid
for my sin on the cross. Forgive me. I open up my whole
life to you. Jesus, come into my life. Fill me with your
Holy Spirit, and make me start again, this time obeying
you, loving you. I give you my life.'